HAROLD S. KUSHNER

Living a Life That Matters

Harold S. Kushner is Rabbi Laureate of
Temple Israel in Natick, Massachusetts,
where he lives. His books include *When
Bad Things Happen to Good People, Who
Needs God,* and *How Good Do We Have
to Be?*

ALSO BY HAROLD S. KUSHNER

How Good Do We Have to Be?

To Life!

Who Needs God

When All You've Ever Wanted Isn't Enough

When Bad Things Happen to Good People

When Children Ask About God

Commanded to Live

Living a Life
That Matters

HAROLD S. KUSHNER

ANCHOR BOOKS
A DIVISION OF RANDOM HOUSE, INC.
NEW YORK

FIRST ANCHOR BOOKS EDITION, SEPTEMBER 2002

Copyright © 2001 by Harold S. Kushner

All rights reserved under International and Pan-American Copyright Conventions.
Published in the United States by Anchor Books, a division of Random House, Inc.,
New York, and simultaneously in Canada by Random House of Canada Limited,
Toronto. Originally published in hardcover in the United States by Alfred A. Knopf,
a division of Random House, Inc., New York, in 2001.

Anchor Books and colophon are registered trademarks of Random House, Inc.

The Library of Congress has cataloged the Knopf edition as follows:
Kushner, Harold S.
Living a life that matters: resolving the conflict between conscience and success / by
Harold Kushner.—1st ed.
p. cm.
ISBN 0-375-41063-5 (alk. paper)
1. Self-esteem—Religious aspects. 2. Meaning (Philosophy)—Religious aspects.
3. Good works (Theology). I. Title.
BL629.5.S44 K87 2001
296.3'6—dc21
2001029874

Anchor ISBN: 0-385-72094-7

Book design by Robert C. Olsson

www.anchorbooks.com

Printed in the United States of America
10 9 8 7 6 5 4 3 2 1

For Chila Sara Haber

The new century is yours. May you see the world
of your dreams realized in your lifetime.

CONTENTS

First Words   ix

ONE: *The Two Voices of God*   3

TWO: *How to Win by Losing*   17

THREE: *What Kind of Person Do
You Want to Be?*   35

FOUR: *Wild Justice: The Seductive Pleasure
of Getting Even*   60

FIVE: *Shalom: The Quest for Integrity*   86

SIX: *Family and Friends: We Are Who We Love*   108

SEVEN: *Best Actor in a Supporting Role*   126

EIGHT: *Why We Matter to the World*   146

Afterword   159

FIRST WORDS

I believe in you. I believe that you have the ability to do great things, things that will change the world for the better. In fact, you may already have done some things—choices you have made, people you have reached out to—that can have big consequences, and you deserve to know that. That is why I have written this book.

Though the book bears only my name on its cover as the author, it is the product of many minds and hands. I have said in previous books how fortunate I have been to have James H. Silberman as my editor. I should add that I believe you, the readers, are equally fortunate that Jim has been my editor. Every page of this book has benefited from his insights and his advice.

Jonathan Segal cast a wise and experienced eye on the manuscript, and I thank him for it.

Once again, my very able agent, Peter Ginsberg of Curtis

Brown Ltd., has been the matchmaker, and I remain deeply grateful to him for that. My wife, Suzette, has been unfailingly supportive when the writing was going well and patient and encouraging when it was going less well. A number of good friends helped me to think through the ideas of this book, and I thank them, too.

Finally, I have dedicated this book to my four-year-old granddaughter, Chila. My two previous books were dedicated to her parents and to her older brother; now it is her turn. Moreover, because she is a second child, "It's my turn" were among Chila's first words, which fits in perfectly with the theme of this book, the human need to know that we are important and that the world takes us seriously. May this book underscore her importance and that of every one of you.

Living a Life That Matters

CHAPTER I

The Two Voices of God

Like many people, I live in two worlds. Much of the time, I live in the world of work and commerce, eating, working, and paying my bills. It is a world that honors people for being attractive and productive. It reveres winners and scorns losers, as reflected in its treatment of devoted public servants who lose an election or in the billboard displayed at the Atlanta Olympic Games a few years ago: "You don't win the silver medal, you lose the gold." As in most contests, there are many more losers than winners, so most of the citizens of that world spend a lot of time worrying that they don't measure up.

But, fortunately, there is another world where, even before I entered it professionally, I have spent some of my time. As a religiously committed person, I live in the world of faith, the world of the spirit. Its heroes are models of compassion rather than competition. In that world, you win through sacrifice and self-restraint. You win by helping your neighbor and sharing with him rather than by finding his weakness and defeating him. And in the world of the spirit, there are many more winners than losers.

When I was young, most of my time and energy were devoted to the world of getting and spending. I relished competition. I wanted to be challenged. How else could I find out how good I was, where I stood on the ladder of winners and losers? I was living out the insight of the psychoanalyst Carl Jung that "act one of a young man's life is the story of his setting out to conquer the world."

Of course, I was not the only person who did that. Most people lived as I did. For several years, our next-door neighbor's son was a nationally renowned professional athlete. It wasn't money that kept him playing and risking serious injury. It was the challenge, the competition, the opportunity to prove once again that he was better than most people at what he did.

When I was young, I saw that second world, the world of faith, as a kind of vacation home, a place to which I repaired in order to relax from the stress of the world of striving, so that I could emerge refreshed to resume the battle. At times, it seemed almost a mirror image of my first world, a place where different people played by different rules. Old people were respected there for their wisdom and experience, as were old ideas and old values. People were described as "beautiful" because they exuded compassion and generosity rather than wealth and glamour. "Success" had a very different meaning there.

As my life increasingly became a story of giving up dreams and coming to terms with my limitations (Jung went on to say, "Act two is the story of a young man realizing that the world is not about to be conquered by the likes of him"), I found myself returning more and more to that second, alternative world. I would often recall the words of my teacher Abraham Joshua Heschel: "When I was young, I admired clever people. As I grew old, I came to admire kind people."

Looking back at my life, I realize that I was commuting between those two worlds in an effort to meet two basic human needs, the need to feel successful and important and the need to think of myself as a good person, someone who deserved the approval of other good people.

We need to know that we matter to the world, that the world takes us seriously. I read a memoir recently in which a woman recalls staying home from school one day as a child because she was sick. Hearing the noises of the world outside her window, she was dismayed to realize that the world was going on without her, not even missing her. The woman grew up to be devoutly religious, a pillar of her church, active in many organizations, feeding the hungry. As I read her story, I wondered if she became an activist to overcome that childhood fear of insignificance, to reassure herself that she *did* make a difference to the world.

In my forty years as a rabbi, I have tended to many people

in the last moments of their lives. Most of them were not afraid of dying. Some were old and felt that they had lived long, satisfying lives. Others were so sick and in such pain that only death would release them. The people who had the most trouble with death were those who felt that they had never done anything worthwhile in their lives, and if God would only give them another two or three years, maybe they would finally get it right. It was not death that frightened them; it was insignificance, the fear that they would die and leave no mark on the world.

The need to feel important drives people to place enormous value on such symbols as titles, corner offices, and first-class travel. It causes us to feel excessively pleased when someone important recognizes us, and to feel hurt when our doctor or pastor passes us on the street without saying hello, or when a neighbor calls us by our sister's or brother's name. The need to know that we are making a difference motivates doctors and medical researchers to spend hours looking through microscopes in the hope of finding cures for diseases. It drives inventors and entrepreneurs to stay up nights trying to find a better way of providing people with something they need. It causes artists, novelists, and composers to try to add to the store of beauty in the world by finding just the right color, the right word, the right note. And it leads ordinary people to buy six copies of the local paper because it has their name or picture in it.

Because we find ourselves in so many settings that proclaim our insignificance—in stores where salespeople don't know our name and don't care to know it, in crowded buses and airplanes that give us the message that if we weren't there someone else would be available to take our place—some people do desperate things to reassure themselves that they matter to the world. I can believe that Lee Harvey Oswald shot President Kennedy and that John Hinckley, Jr., tried to kill President Reagan in large measure to prove that the world was wrong in not taking them seriously. They had the power to change history. At a less crucial level, there are people who confuse notoriety with celebrity, and celebrity with importance. They go to extreme lengths to get their names in the *Guinness Book of Records,* or to appear on daytime television shows, revealing things about themselves and their families that most of us would be embarrassed to reveal to our clergyman or our closest friends. They may come across as pitiable; the audience may scorn them. But for one hour their story holds the attention of millions of Americans. They matter.

At the same time, we need to be assured that we are good people. A few years ago, I wrote a book entitled *How Good Do We Have to Be?* Its basic message was that God does not expect perfection from us, so we should not demand perfection of ourselves or those around us, for God knows what a complicated story a human life is and loves us despite our inevitable lapses. As I traveled around the country talking about my book, something interesting kept happening.

Although most people in my audience welcomed the message that God loved them despite their mistakes and failings, in every audience there would be a significant number of people who were uncomfortable with it. They wanted to believe that God loved them, and other people loved them, because they *deserved* it, not because God and the other people in their lives were gracious enough to put up with them. They wanted to believe that God cared about the choices they made every day, choosing between selfishness and generosity, between honesty and deceitfulness, and that the world became a better place when they made the right choices. They were like the college student who hands in a paper and wants the professor to read it carefully and critically, because he or she has worked so hard to make it good. The people in my audience felt that they had worked hard to lead moral lives. They might hope that God would make allowances for human frailty, but, like the college student, they would be sorely disappointed by the response, That's all right, I really didn't expect much from you anyway.

My answer to them when they challenged me was that I believe God speaks to us in two voices.

One is the stern, commanding voice issuing from the mountaintop, thundering "Thou shalt not!," summoning us to be more, to reach higher, to demand greater things of ourselves, forbidding us to use the excuse "I'm only human," because to be human is a wondrous thing.

God's other voice is the voice of compassion and forgiveness, an embracing, cleansing voice, assuring us that when we have aimed high and fallen short we are still loved. God understands that when we give in to temptation it is a temporary lapse and does not reflect our true character.

Some years ago, Erich Fromm wrote a little book entitled *The Art of Loving,* in which he distinguished between what he called "mother love" and "father love" (emphasizing that people of either gender are capable of both kinds of love). Mother love says: You are bone of my bone and flesh of my flesh, and I will always love you no matter what. Nothing you ever do or fail to do will make me stop loving you. Father love says: I will love you if you *earn* my love and respect, if you get good grades, if you make the team, if you get into a good college, earn a good salary.

Fromm insists that every one of us needs to experience both kinds of loving. It may seem at first glance that mother love is good, warm, and freely given, father love harsh and conditional (I will only love you if . . .). But as my audiences taught me, and as a moment's reflection might teach us all, sometimes we want to hear the father's message that we are loved because we deserve it, not only because the other person is so generous and tolerant.

People need to hear the same message from God that children need to hear from their earthly parents. Just as it is an unforgettably comforting and necessary experience for a child caught doing something wrong to be forgiven and to learn that parental love is a gift that will not be arbitrarily withdrawn, a lesson no child should grow up without absorbing, so is it a vital part of everyone's religious upbringing to learn that God's love is not tentative, that our failures do not alienate us from God. That is why Roman Catholic churches offer the sacrament of confession and penance, why Protestant liturgy emphasizes that the church is a home for imperfect people, and why Yom Kippur, the Day of Atonement for our sins, is the holiest day of the Jewish calendar.

When we are feeling burdened by guilt, when we know that we have done wrong and hate ourselves for it, we need to hear the voice of God-as-mother, assuring us that nothing can alienate us from God's love. But when we have worked hard to be good, honest, generous people, there is something lacking in the message, I love you despite yourself because I am so loving and lenient. What is missing is the voice of God-as-father: You're good, you have earned My love.

I can't tell you how many men and women I have counseled who spent their entire adult lives feeling somehow incomplete and unsure of their worth because they never heard their father tell them, You're good and I love you for it. I once paid a condolence call on a man in my congregation whose father had just died. The funeral and memorial week had taken place in another city, where his parents had lived, and I was the only visitor on his first night home. After several minutes of asking about the funeral and how his mother was coping, I found myself saying, "It sounds like your father was a man who kept his emotions to himself."

The congregant broke down and started to cry. "He never said anything good about me. All my life, I wanted to hear him say he was proud of me for who I was and what I was doing, and all I ever got from him was this sense that he showed his love by putting up with me." He wiped his eyes, apologized for the tears, and went on. "In my head, I know that he had a problem talking about his feelings. In my head, I know he thought his way was the right way to make me do better. But in my heart, I feel so cheated. I always got good grades in school, never got into trouble, went to a good college. I make a good living, live in a nice home, have a wonderful family. Would it have been so hard for him just once to tell me that he was proud of me? And now he's dead and I'll never hear it!"

I tried to tell him that the problem was his father's, not his, that his father was part of an older generation of men who had trouble knowing what they were feeling, let alone putting it into words. I reminded him that his father had grown up in the 1930s, during the hard years of the Depression, and had probably been forced by circumstance to grow a hard outer shell over his sensitive inner core, because sensitive, caring people were often left behind in those years. I prompted him to remember all the nonverbal ways in which his father had shown love and concern for him. But I don't know how much that helped. My congregant may be a permanent member of that army of men and women who will always feel a little bit incomplete because they never got the message of father love—I love you for what you have made of yourself—and will keep on working and struggling until someone they care about tells them that.

People need to hear the message that they are good. And people who are not entirely sure of their goodness may need that validation even more. That may be why churches and synagogues attract people who are bothered by the lapses in their behavior as husbands and wives, as parents, and as children of aging parents, and crave the reassurance that they are welcome in God's house. That may be why a wealthy businessman cherishes a twenty-five-dollar plaque given him by his church, synagogue, or lodge for being honored as Man of the Year. It may explain why we do things that don't benefit us economically but benefit us psychologically: making charitable donations, volunteering for good causes. We do them to nourish our self-image as generous, caring people. I have met many people who joined the local Rotary Club or Young Presidents Organization to make useful contacts, but stayed and became active because they came to enjoy the feeling of making their community a better place. And it may be why we make excuses for the things we do that embarrass us. How do most of us handle our mistakes? We blame others, we blame our upbringing, we rationalize what we did, in an effort to reassure ourselves of our essential goodness. (Our rationalizations do seem aimed at ourselves; they rarely persuade anyone else.) In his book *Three Seductive Ideas,*

Dr. Jerome Kagan, professor of psychology at Harvard, writes, "The desire to believe that the self is ethically worthy . . . is universal." He points out that children as young as two years old evaluate their behavior in terms of right and wrong and need to think of themselves as good. Without that innate moral sense, Kagan believes, children could not be socialized.

We tend to assume that people who violate the law in a serious way—violent criminals, gang members, bank robbers—are immoral people, people who don't care about society's rules or what others think of them. But a psychologist friend of mine who has spent time working with prisoners in a federal penitentiary learned something different. He told me that when he started he assumed that he would be dealing with hardened criminals, people who were indifferent to moral obligations and considerations of right and wrong. To his surprise, he learned that prison inmates hold to a very strict moral code. It may not be our moral code; it may not be a moral code we would find admirable or even acceptable. But in the prison setting, there is behavior for which you gain approval (not ratting on associates) and there is behavior that sinks you to the bottom of the moral pecking order (imprisonment for hurting women or children). Similarly, gang members may appear to us as having total disregard for moral considerations and public opinion, but within the gang, they will risk injury and hardship to live up to its rules. Apparently, even people on the fringes of society (or well beyond the fringe) cannot bear to think of themselves as bad people. They will insist on their innocence, they will blame the circumstances of their growing up, or they will defend the morality of what they do. In Mario Puzo's novel *The Godfather,* Michael Corleone says of his father, Don Vito, "He operates on a code of ethics he considers far superior to the legal strictures of society."

We human beings are such complicated creatures. We have so many needs, so many emotional hungers, and they often come into conflict with each other. Our impulse to help needy people or support medical research conflicts with our desire to have the money to buy all the things we are attracted to. My commitment to doing the right thing impels me to want to apologize to people I have offended, but my desire to protect my image and nourish my sense of righteousness persuades me that the problem is their hypersensitivity, not my behavior. What happens when our need to think of ourselves as good people collides with our need to be recognized as important? Is it possible to do both? How often do we find ourselves betraying our values, violating our consciences, in our struggle to have an impact on the world? Political candidates compromise their values to raise funds and gain votes. Salesmen exaggerate the virtues of their wares. Doctors, lawyers, and businessmen neglect their families in the pursuit of professional and financial success. Often we don't like what we find ourselves doing (although it is remarkable how easily we get used to it after the first few times), but we tell ourselves we have no choice. That is the kind of world we live in, and that is the price we have to pay for claiming our space in it.

This may well be the central dilemma in the lives of many of us. We want—indeed, we need—to think of ourselves as good people, though from time to time we find ourselves doing things that make us doubt our goodness. We dream of leaving the world a better place for our having passed through it, though we often wonder whether, in our quest for significance, we litter the world with our mistakes more than we bless it with our accomplishments. Our souls are split, part of us reaching for goodness, part of us chasing fame and fortune and doing questionable things along the way, as we realize that those two paths may diverge sharply. Our self-image is like an out-of-focus photograph, two slightly blurred images instead of one clear one. Much of our lives, much of our energy will be devoted to closing that gap between the longings of our soul and the scoldings of our conscience, between our too-often conflicting needs for the assurance of knowing that we are good and the satisfaction of being told that we are important.

The people we find ourselves admiring most tend to be people who strike us as having closed that gap, having resolved that conflict. Many of the biographies we read, and especially the life story to which we will turn in the next chapter, are accounts of people struggling to reconcile those two longings, to be good and to matter. We examine their lives, not only to gain information but to gain insight as to how they managed to do that, in the hope that we too will be able to gain the two prizes for which our souls yearn.

CHAPTER 2

How to Win by Losing

He was alone. The night was totally dark and he was afraid. He tried to calm his fears by repeating to himself that he was alone and that, as long as he was alone, nothing bad could happen to him. Suddenly someone seized him from behind and threw him to the ground. He tried to fight back. He had worked hard all his life and he was strong, but his adversary was just as strong as he was. They fought and struggled and wrestled through the night, neither one able to gain an advantage over the other. Who is this person, the man wondered, who is exactly as strong as I am? Where did he come from and what does he want with me? Then, as the first rays of dawn began to appear, he felt the mysterious stranger twist his leg and escape from his grip. The two men, sweating and exhausted, regarded each other with the grudging respect men have for worthy adversaries whom they cannot defeat.

The man knew he would never again be the same person he had been until just a few hours before.

The story could be taken from the files of a city police station, or told by a soldier on sentry duty. It could have happened last week or a thousand years ago. But it is from the Bible, from the thirty-second chapter of the book of Genesis. It is the story of how Jacob wrestled with an angel and how his name came to be changed from Jacob, "the trickster," to Israel, "one who struggles with God."

Jacob may be the most intriguing person in the Bible. We know more about him than about virtually any other biblical character. More chapters of Genesis are devoted to Jacob and his family than to any of the other patriarchs. He is the only person in the Bible whom we see in action as a child, a young man, a mature husband and father, and an old man contemplating death. We see him interacting with his parents, his brother, his wives, his father-in-law, his children, and his grandchildren, as well as with the God of his ancestors. If we read the biographies of good people in an effort to learn how to achieve goodness ourselves, if we study the lives of people who mattered so that we can learn how to make our own lives matter, and if we recognize the Bible as the repository of more wisdom about what it means to live in the presence of God than any other book ever written, we can do no better than to seek to understand the story of Jacob and what it can teach us.

It all began with his grandfather Abraham, who came to

the revolutionary conclusion that behind everything stands a single God, not many gods, and that this God demands righteous behavior of human beings. Abraham and his wife, Sarah, passed this belief on to Isaac, their only child in common. Isaac and his wife, Rebecca, had twin sons, Jacob and Esau, born after a difficult pregnancy in which Rebecca felt the two babies struggling with each other inside her, foreshadowing the struggles that would mark their lives. Esau, the eldest by a matter of minutes, was a coarse, physical brute of a man, a hunter. Jacob, who was born holding on to his brother's heel (hence the name Jacob—tripper-upper, trickster), was quieter.

As so often in tales of twin brothers, they were opposites in many ways, almost as if each were half of a complete personality, as if in the womb each brother had grabbed half the available traits and left the other half to his twin. Esau was a man of few words. When he spoke, he would utter only a few short syllables. Jacob was more thoughtful and articulate. Esau was his father's favorite, perhaps because he was the strong, physical man his father had always wanted to be and never was, like a desk-bound father of today who lives vicariously through his athletic son. Jacob was his mother's favorite, perhaps because she saw more of herself in him while wondering what had made Esau so different from either of his parents.

In one encounter that teaches us much about the character of the two brothers, Esau comes home from an unsuccessful day of hunting, finds Jacob cooking lentil stew, and, desperately hungry, asks his brother for some. Jacob trades the bowl of stew for Esau's birthright, that Jacob be considered the firstborn son and thus receive the greater portion of their father's estate after his death. In that brief exchange, just six verses at the end of chapter 25 of Genesis, we see Esau defined as a man ruled by appetites, a man who lives for the moment with no regard for tomorrow. "What good is a birthright if I die of hunger today?" he says, as if people died as a result of missing a meal! And we see Jacob's scheming side, a young man who will try to get by cleverness what he cannot get by birth or strength.

The young Jacob belongs to the literary tradition of the trickster, the hero who defeats his opponents by cleverness rather than by strength, a tradition that includes the Norse god Loki, Homer's Odysseus (usually referred to as "crafty" or "wily" Odysseus), and the heroes of folktales in so many cultures. What makes Jacob unique in that tradition is the Bible's ambivalence about his tricks. The Norse myths never question Loki's winning by guile, nor does Homer ever see Odysseus as less than heroic, but as we will see, the Bible is uncomfortable with Jacob's cleverness.

I once heard a psychologist contrast two styles of morality. There is the morality of cleverness and wit, in which success means getting the better of the other person by means of a slick business deal or a clever answer, the worst sin is letting someone take advantage of you (think of Woody Allen's line

"In my family, the worst sin was paying retail"), and the worst punishment is shame, having other people think less of you for having been bettered. Then there is the morality of righteousness, in which the highest good is thoughtfulness toward others, the worst sin is hurting another person, and the worst punishment is guilt, thinking less of yourself for what you have done. Jacob's story is the story of his evolution from the first kind of morality to the second, and in this book we will be drawn to Jacob's story because we will recognize that same struggle, that same growth in our own lives.

As the biblical story continues, Isaac has become old and blind, and believes he does not have very much longer to live (though he will in fact live another twenty-five years). He is prepared to bestow the patriarchal blessing on his favored son, Esau, designating him as the one who will continue the family traditions. The implication is that Isaac's blindness is spiritual as much as it is physical. He cannot see that Jacob, for all his limitations, is the more qualified.

Rebecca sees that all too clearly, and devises an elaborate scheme to make sure that the right brother is blessed. She dresses Jacob in Esau's clothes, covers his hairless arms with goatskins so that he will feel and smell like Esau, and sends him in to his blind father to be blessed before Esau gets back from the field. Though Jacob is uncomfortable with the ruse, more out of fear of being caught than out of a sense that it is wrong, he carries it out. He tricks his father into blessing him. But we are beginning to see the split in Jacob's soul, the inner conflict between his desire to get what he desperately wants and the sense that he can get it only by doing something deceitful and disliking himself for it. This split will deepen with time and will come to a head in his nighttime struggle with the angel.

Jacob's behavior makes many readers uncomfortable. We know that he is the hero of the story. We know that Rebecca is right and Jacob is more qualified than Esau to be the heir to Abraham's legacy. But we are uncomfortable with his gaining a spiritual blessing by such devious means. We would like our heroes to be more heroic, so that we can believe that we too can follow the high road to success. In the course of my studies, I found a fascinating psychological interpretation of the incident in a nineteenth-century commentary by an East European Hasidic rabbi who had never heard of Sigmund Freud but knew something about how the human soul works. The rabbi suggests that when Jacob tells his father, "I am Esau," he is not simply lying. At some level, he wants to be Esau. He envies his brother's physical strength and hunter's skills. He realizes that, as a twin, he is in some ways an incomplete person, and he wants to become whole by assuming Esau's identity along with his own. Esau, by contrast, never shows any interest in acquiring Jacob's more cerebral gifts.

The ruse works for only a few minutes. Esau arrives and exposes his brother as living up to his name, the trickster/tripper-upper, but it is too late. The blessing, once given, cannot be withdrawn. Furious, Esau threatens to kill Jacob, and Jacob prudently takes his mother's advice and flees to the home of his maternal uncle Laban in another country.

On his first night away from home, Jacob, a frightened adolescent ashamed of what he has done, goes to sleep on the desert floor and has a dream. He dreams of a ladder reaching from earth to heaven. At the top of the ladder, he senses (rather than sees) God, who assures him that his life will turn out well, that he will one day return home safely and go on to be a special person and do great things. The symbol of the ladder will be an important theme in Jacob's life. When we first get to know him, there is a lot about him that is not very likable. But what fascinates us about Jacob, and what makes the story of his life a story that can teach us, is that he is a person who grows. If the ladder that bridges heaven and earth represents the distance between Jacob as he is and Jacob as he would like to be, then his life story is the account of his struggle to climb that ladder, to ascend from a lower level of behavior to a higher one, and to become a more complete person not through disguise and misrepresentation but through sacrifice and growth.

No matter whether dreams come from God and foretell the future or well up from the wishes of our subconscious, Jacob's dream must have been immensely reassuring to him. He awakens and prays to God, promising that if God will indeed watch over him and bring him home safely he will offer to God a tithe, 10 percent of everything he ever earns.

Jacob continues on foot to the land of Aram (known today as Syria), where his uncle lives. At the well at the entrance to Laban's town, Jacob meets his cousin Rachel and falls in love with her. Jacob is the first person in the Bible to be described as falling in love with a woman and wanting to marry her. Previous references are to men "taking" wives. Isaac, for example, is described as learning to love his wife Rebecca only after their arranged marriage.

Jacob wants to marry Rachel, but, without money or prospects, he cannot pay the bride price her family expects. (In agricultural societies, the suitor had to compensate the bride's family for depriving them of a working hand. Later, in commercial societies where young women did not work the fields, the bride's family would pay a dowry to the man who offered to take their daughter and support her.) Jacob offers to work seven years for his uncle Laban at no wages to earn Rachel's hand in marriage.

On the wedding night, after everyone has had a lot to drink, Laban craftily substitutes his older, less attractive daughter, Leah, for Rachel. The next morning, when Jacob discovers the deception and complains, Laban replies, "I understand that there are some places where the younger child rushes ahead of the older, but we would never let that happen here." Jacob, who had fooled his father as Laban has fooled him, has no comeback. He has just learned what it feels like to be the victim of a clever man's trickery and now understands why it is wrong to lie and cheat: What kind of life can a person have in a world where he can't trust anyone?

Jacob is permitted to marry Rachel only after promising another seven years of labor. His two wives bear him several children, most born to Leah. Rachel, like Sarah and Rebecca before her, has difficulty conceiving, a common motif in ancient tales to forecast that the child born after years of longing will grow up to be special. Laban's flocks and herds flourish and increase under Jacob's care, and both men become wealthy. After some years, Jacob comes to feel that it is time for him to take his family and his flocks and go home. Concerned that Laban will again try to cheat him, Jacob leaves secretly while Laban is away shearing his sheep. Laban pursues him and catches up to him at the border between Aram and Canaan. Jacob reminds Laban of how faithfully he has served him and how often Laban has tried to cheat him. Laban extracts from Jacob a promise to treat his wives, Laban's daughters, with due consideration, and they come to an amicable parting. Jacob is now ready to cross the river into Canaan and head for home. He sends the women, children, and animals across and, as night falls, is left alone on the far side of the river. It is then and there that the mysterious night figure attacks him and struggles with him until daybreak.

Who is this mysterious being? Why does he attack Jacob, and why do they fight to a standoff? Most commentaries see him as a malign figure, a dangerous enemy seeking to harm Jacob. Some see him as Esau's guardian angel, others as a demon who guards the boundary that separates the two countries and seeks to prevent people from crossing. Still others see him as the personification of all the dangers lurking in darkness.

I have always interpreted the story differently. I see the mysterious attacker as part of Jacob himself. That is why he appears when the Bible emphasizes that Jacob is alone. That is why he is exactly as strong as Jacob, no stronger, no weaker. The attacker, the angel, is Jacob's conscience, the part of him that summons him to rise above his bad impulses. The struggle is between the part of him that wins by cleverness and fraud, and the part of him that feels summoned by God to climb a ladder to heaven, to become someone exemplary.

Jacob is at war with himself. Part of him takes pride in his ability to use his cleverness to fool people and get what he wants. But another part of him is uncomfortable with all that cleverness and the realization that people resent and mistrust him for it.

Remember the situation: Jacob is about to return home after having fled in disgrace. The next day he expects to see his brother Esau for the first time in twenty years. Jacob undoubtedly remembers Esau's parting words: "The next time I see you, I'll kill you because of what you did to me." I can imagine Jacob trying to come up with some clever plan to evade the confrontation, and then saying to himself, No! All my life, whenever I have been in difficulty, I have responded by lying and running away. I hate myself for being a person who lies and runs. I wish I were brave enough to face up to the consequences of my behavior, but every time I try, I back off. I'm afraid of meeting Esau tomorrow, but I'm equally afraid of continuing the pattern of trying to solve problems by being devious.

We know that Jacob loves Rachel, but at one point, the Bible tells us that he hates Leah. It has been suggested that he hates Leah because every time he sees her he is reminded of how he was tricked into marrying her, and that in turn reminds him of how he tricked his father into blessing him. He can't escape from the daily reminder of the lowest point in his life, the day he alienated himself from his family and began to think less of himself as a person. How often do we hate people not because of who they are or what they do, but because they remind us of something we dislike in ourselves, something we would rather not be reminded of? Jung writes of what he calls "the shadow," the negative side of our personalities, those aspects of ourselves that we don't like and would rather pretend are not really there. But the more we try to put them behind us and keep them out of sight, the more they follow us around like our shadows.

I think many of us can identify with Jacob's struggle, symbolized in the biblical narrative as wrestling with an angel. There are times when we feel that split inside us, part of us wanting to take the easy way out even as another part of us insists on taking the more demanding route, part of us wanting to give money to the beggar or write a check to charity while another part gives us reasons to keep the money for ourselves, part of us wanting to play the Good Samaritan and stop to help someone in need while a voice inside our head urges us not to get involved. There are times when we scold ourselves, How could you do that? Didn't you know it was wrong? or warn ourselves, Stop right now and don't go any further, before you get into trouble. We know how easy it is, with practice, to ignore the voice of conscience. The Talmud says that at first a bad habit enters our lives as an invited guest but before long it becomes a member of the family and ultimately ends up taking over the house, and we come to feel that we have lost a precious part of who we are and who we want to be.

Like Jacob, we know what it feels like to try to climb higher on the ladder, only to experience a fear of heights and a yearning for the familiar feeling of solid ground under our feet. We revert to the old habits and think less of ourselves for doing so.

Who wins this epic wrestling match between Jacob and his conscience? Since the two antagonists are both aspects of the same man, we can understand that Jacob wins and also loses. At the end of the struggle, Jacob is injured and limping, but the Bible nonetheless describes him as *shalem,* a Hebrew word with connotations of wholeness, integrity, being at peace with oneself. The word is related to *shalom,* peace. In a sense, Jacob has won by losing. Until now, whenever Jacob has had pangs of conscience—when he traded a bowl of stew for his brother's birthright instead of simply sharing it with his hungry brother, when he misrepresented himself to gain a blessing from his blind father, when he favored one of his wives over the other—he has always been able to defeat his conscience, to rationalize his behavior, to silence the voice inside him that warned him that he was doing wrong. Paradoxically, the weaker a person he was, the easier it was for him to defeat his conscience. He never felt strong enough, secure enough to do the right thing when doing right seemed hard. Only when he had climbed partway up the ladder that leads from earth to heaven, only when marriage and fatherhood and the experience of being cheated by others had gained him a measure of maturity, was he strong enough to let his conscience hold its own against him. He is no longer Jacob the trickster, the conniver. He will become Israel, the one who struggles with God and with men (that is, with his conscience and with his less honorable nature). In the richly nuanced Hebrew of the biblical narrative, the name Jacob has connotations of *akov,* crooked, whereas Israel has echoes of *yashar,* straight.

Do you remember Jacob's prayer on his first night away from home, right after his dream of the ladder? Jacob asked God to protect him and bring him home safely, and promised to tithe his earnings if God would do that. On this, his last night before re-entering Canaan, moments before the angel attacks him, Jacob prays again. But this time there are no promises, no bargaining with God. This time Jacob says to God, You have already done more for me than I had any right to expect. I have nothing to offer You in return. All I can say is this: I am turning to You because I need You. I have to do something tomorrow and I'm not sure I'm up to it. It's something I have never been strong enough to do before. But if You are with me, maybe I can manage it. You once promised me, on my first night away from home, that I would grow up to be a special person. For that promise to come true, You need to help me tomorrow.

Jacob doesn't ask God to solve his problems for him. He doesn't ask God to strike Esau with amnesia so that he will no longer be angry with him. He doesn't pray for a clever idea to fool Esau into forgiving him. He prays for the strength to do the right thing. It is immediately after that that the angel seizes him.

Jacob is wounded in his struggle with the angel. Perhaps the most important lesson Jacob learns that night is that he can be hurt but can survive the hurt. He can pay the price of honesty, of generosity, and, yes, it will hurt, but he will get over it. About physical wounds, physician and best-selling author Dr. Rachel Naomi Remen has written, "How might you live if you did not know that your body could heal? Would you ever ride your bike, drive a car, use a knife to cut up vegetables? Or would you never get off the couch?" But

Jacob's night wound is emotional as well as physical. For the first time in his life, he will let himself be forced to do the right thing, to face up to his brother and try to atone for having cheated him rather than use his wits to avoid a confrontation or excuse his behavior. He knows it will hurt, but just as he has learned to trust his body to heal from its wounds, he is prepared to trust his soul to recover from the pain of doing something difficult. He puts his faith in the belief that doing the right thing is the best medicine for a troubled soul.

At one point in Jacob's nighttime struggle, his mysterious opponent asks him, "What is your name?" It seems like a strange question to ask in the middle of a fight, but in ancient times a name was more than an identifying label. It pointed to a person's identity. "Who are you?" really meant, What kind of person are you? What values do you live by?—not just, What do people call you? If Jacob is wrestling with his conscience, his better self, then asking himself, What is my name? is his way of asking, Who am I really? What kind of person do I want to be? I know who I have been until now; who do I want to be from now on?

I find it significant that at the end of the wrestling encounter God gives Jacob a new name. What does it mean when a person changes his or her name? I have known people who changed their names, changed their religion, changed their jobs, or moved to a different state as a way of saying that they didn't want to continue being who they had been to that point. When a professional athlete converts to Islam and takes on a new name, when a Jew decides to become observant and asks people to call him by his Hebrew name ("I'm no longer Charles, I'm Chaim"), what are they saying about who they used to be and who they are now? When a woman, upon marriage, chooses to take her husband's last name, or to keep her family name, or to use both names hyphenated, what is she saying about the extent to which marriage redefines her sense of who she is? Once, when a prospective bride told me that she would be using her fiancé's surname after marriage, I expressed mild surprise. I said to her, "I had the impression you were a staunch feminist." She answered, "I am. If I'm to be known by some guy's name, I'd rather it be the guy I chose than the guy my mother chose."

In the Bible, it is God who changes Jacob's name to Israel, which I understand as symbolizing the victory of his conscience, his better nature, in the battle to define what kind of person Jacob will become. In the struggle over Jacob's soul, the angel has won.

It hurt Jacob to lose his battle with the angel, but it would have hurt him more had he kept on winning. Dr. Remen writes of a patient who experienced chest pains that neither medication nor meditation nor surgery could alleviate. One day the patient realized that she experienced the pain whenever she was about to do something she didn't really believe in, something that lacked integrity and compromised her most deeply held values. That was her angel attacking her. Dr. Remen suspected that "the loss of emotional or spiritual integrity may be at the source of our suffering conscience. . . . Stress (which can affect us physically) may be as much a question of a compromise of values as it is a matter of time pressure and fear of failure."

It hurts to be defeated by conscience, to feel compelled to take the more demanding high road, to resist temptation, to apologize. But I suspect it hurts more to keep winning out over conscience. Too often, we compromise our integrity, we do something we really don't believe in doing, to reach some important goal, only to find one of two frustrating things happening: Either we gain the prize and realize it wasn't worth gaining, or we end up with neither the prize nor our integrity.

On that dark night on the bank of the river, Jacob's desire to be successful, to get what he wanted in life by whatever means it took, came into conflict with his growing need to think of himself as a good person. He tried to fool his conscience, to quiet his conscience, to debate and persuade his conscience. But for the first time in his life, Jacob's conscience was strong enough to stand up to him. This time, it would not be stared down. It would not be talked into something. It would not be defeated. Like so many moments we dread, like so many things we are not sure we are capable of doing, the actual confrontation turned out to be a lot easier than Jacob feared it would be. And Jacob, to his astonishment, found that he liked himself better when his conscience prevailed against him.

When we defeat the still, small voice of God inside us, we lose. But that voice inside us will not be stilled forever (and God help the person who does succeed in permanently stilling the voice of his conscience). It will find a time when we are vulnerable. It will attack us at a weak moment. And when the struggle is over, we will, like Jacob/Israel, be bruised and limping. But, again like Jacob, we will be whole, we will be at peace with ourselves, in a way we never were before.

CHAPTER 3

What Kind of Person Do You Want to Be?

Why do good people do bad things? If we all have an innate need to think of ourselves as good, why do we do things that undercut our sense of our own goodness? When I read the story of Jacob's nighttime struggle, I identify with him, because I too have known the feeling of doing things that I didn't believe in and thinking less of myself for it.

I met with a husband and wife, members of my congregation, to talk about a problem they were having. I knew the couple and liked them. I had performed their wedding twenty years earlier, and had watched their children grow up. I was worried about what might be troubling them: marital problems? conflicts with their teenagers at home? It turned out that it wasn't a family matter at all. It concerned their business. Some years before, they had taken in a partner. It had recently become clear to them that this man was dishonest and had been systematically cheating them. One of them said to me, "It's not the money; we're in good shape. And we're not asking you for legal advice; we have good lawyers. What bothers us is this: We trusted this man because he was a religious Jew. How can a person be so scrupulous about what he eats and when he prays, and then do something like this to people who trusted him?"

That same evening, my wife and I had dinner with a friend. When it came time for coffee and dessert, our friend declined, explaining that she had to be in court early the next morning. She was suing a lawyer for defrauding her in a real-estate transaction. "What's so upsetting," she told us, "is that I went to him in the first place because I felt I could trust him. He's a deacon of our church. How could somebody like that turn around and do something so flagrantly dishonest?"

I tried to tell the couple in my office and our friend at the restaurant that organized religion attracts all sorts of people, good and bad, strong and weak, for all sorts of reasons. I quoted a line I had once written, that a church or synagogue that only admitted saints would be like a hospital that only admitted healthy people. It would be a more pleasant place and easier to run, but that's not what we're in business for.

I don't know if my words satisfied my friends, but they didn't entirely convince me. I was left wondering about all the people I have met over the years whose personal and professional behavior was so disconnected from the faith they professed. I know many people who have lost faith in organized religion because they have met ostensibly religious people, clergy and laymen, whose behavior did not match the badges of piety they so conspicuously wore. Why is this so common?

Some people embrace a religious life out of a desire to live at the highest moral level, to exult in spending every waking moment conscious of the presence of God. But there are others who commit themselves to a religious life because they, like Jacob in the Bible, are troubled when they find themselves doing things they know are wrong. Like Jacob, they give in to temptation. They lie rather than tell the truth. They take shortcuts, gaining by cleverness and fraud what they want and cannot get by honesty. And, like Jacob, at some level they hate themselves for it. They are not hypocrites, professing one thing while really believing another. They truly believe what their religious faith tells them, but time and again they find themselves acting in ways contrary to what they believe. Their level of public religious observance may be intended to reassure themselves that they are not all bad, to quiet the nagging voice of conscience and gain the reassurance that they really are acceptable in the sight of God.

Some people use religion to strengthen their immune systems and help them resist temptation. Some use it as an antibiotic to cleanse their systems of infection and make them feel healthy again. And some use it as an aspirin, to take away the pain of wrongdoing without affecting the cause of that pain.

Some years ago, I had a friend, a Protestant minister in a nearby town, who was the most dedicated clergyman I have ever known. He was an indefatigable pastor to the sick, the elderly, the grieving in his congregation. He was a force for good in the community, in interfaith and interracial activities. He was as much at home on the church softball or bowling team as in the pulpit. I often wished we had someone like him in our community. Then, one day, I heard that he had resigned from the church and was moving away. It seems that he had been caught behaving inappropriately with some young girls in the church youth group. I invited him to lunch, to let him know that not everyone was afraid to be seen with him. I told him how much I had always admired his pastoral work. He answered, "Yes, I worked very hard as a pastor, so that if this other side of me ever came out people would at least have something good to remember about me."

Was he a good or a bad man? The parents of the girls he molested likely think of him as a monster and a hypocrite. But to this day, I find myself thinking of him sadly as a good man tormented by urges he knew were wrong but could not control. I find myself wondering if, when he reads his Bible and comes to the story of Jacob's struggle with the angel, he takes the story personally and wishes that he had let the angel win more often.

Why do people do things that should be easy to recognize as unacceptable? Are people naturally bad, and is good behavior only a thin veneer, the result of social pressure and the fear of being caught? No doubt there are some truly evil people in the world, but probably fewer than we think there are. Hitler, Stalin, Charles Manson, and some other serial killers make the list; most people who do bad things probably don't. People like Hitler and Stalin are psychopaths, and I am as baffled by their lack of conscience as everyone else is. That may be why there are more biographies of Hitler, by writers trying to make sense of his life, than there are of Mother Teresa. It may be that some people are born without the ability to develop a fully functioning conscience, in the same way that some people are born with a malfunctioning limb or organ or lacking an enzyme that is necessary for normal life. Or it may be that some people are so irreparably crippled by childhood experiences that they grow up emotionally deformed. They have been described as being like mad dogs. You can't reason with them, and you can't change them; you can only try to stay out of their way. I remember the day I had to tell my young children not to take candy from strangers or get into a stranger's car. They had spent their early years in a protected environment, surrounded by people who loved them, and they had learned, as all children deserve to learn, to trust the world. Now I had to explain to them that there were bad people in the world who like to hurt children. They asked me "Why?" and I had no answer for them. The bullies, perverts, and criminals I was warning them about had been born innocent babies themselves. What had led them astray? And I am equally baffled by what goes into the making of a saint, a strikingly wonderful person virtually free of the moral compromises in which the rest of us find ourselves entangled.

If we think of all the people in the world spread along a continuum of virtue, there will be a few saints at one end and some truly horrible people at the other. Closer to the sinners' end, we will find people so angry at the world that they feel entitled to hurt others, people so focused on their own feelings that they don't care about the feelings of those they cheat and betray. Closer to the saints' end of the continuum, we find people more like ourselves, good people who sometimes do bad things for reasons we don't entirely understand.

What makes good people like us, basically decent people, violate our own sincerely held moral standards? What made Jacob deceive his father, or King David seduce another man's wife, as described in chapter 11 of the second book of Samuel?

Sometimes we choose to do the wrong thing because we are afraid and feel that we have to protect ourselves. An honest man, if he is hungry enough, will steal food or the money to buy food. He will be manifestly uncomfortable doing it, but that will probably not make much of a difference to the person he is stealing from. A pacifist may use a weapon against someone who is endangering his family, even though he will feel morally compromised doing so. In chapter 12 of Genesis, we find Abraham treating his wife, Sarah, disgracefully. Because of a drought in Canaan, there is no grass for his flocks. So Abraham and Sarah journey to Egypt, where the Nile River keeps the pastures green. Abraham fears that they are entering a society that abuses strangers, that the Egyptians will kill him in order to take Sarah for themselves. So he asks Sarah to pose as his unmarried sister, not his wife. Though she may be violated, his life will be saved. Only God's intervention allows them to leave Egypt alive with Sarah's virtue intact. It is troubling to find a paragon of virtue like Abraham, the founder of monotheism and the father of three great world religions, acting in so cowardly and selfish a fashion. But the lesson may be that fear for one's life can drive even someone like Abraham to compromise his standards. Or, conversely, a person who lies and connives in situations of stress and danger can also be a person who does wondrous things and changes the world for the better during the greater part of his life, when he or she is not feeling threatened. I have seen survivors of Hitler's death camps, good, generous, compassionate people who after the war became exemplary husbands, wives, and parents, shed tears of shame when they remembered the things they had to do to stay alive in those inhuman circumstances. Few of us would ever pass judgment on them.

Sometimes good people do things they don't believe in because they believe that the end justifies the means. Jacob may well have felt that he, not Esau, deserved his father's blessing. It would have made a mockery of everything Abraham represented for Esau to be his designated heir. So Jacob felt justified when he disguised himself and deceived his father. A political candidate whose life is rooted in honesty and integrity may give himself permission to distort his opponent's record because he sincerely believes that his opponent's election would be a disaster for his community. A college admissions officer may bend the rules to admit an academically unqualified student who is a star athlete so that a winning football team will gain favorable publicity for the school. A lawyer may hide facts, badger witnesses, and appeal to jurors' emotions in order to bring about a verdict that he believes justice requires.

In all of these instances, the people will be troubled by what they did, as Jacob was. They will most likely pray that no one finds out about it. It won't be that hard for them to convince themselves that what they did was a necessary compromise in a world that can't always be counted on to be fair. But the split in their souls between what they believe and what they practice will be there, and because they are basically good, moral people, this will disturb them.

It is important for us to remember, though we don't often stop to reflect on it, that only good people feel guilty. Evil people rarely feel guilty. They deny, they justify, they rationalize, they blame others without accepting their share of responsibility. Only morally sensitive people struggle with the gap between who they are and who they know they ought to be.

Sometimes good people do wrong because doing what they know to be right is too hard for them, or because the advantage to be gained by taking a shortcut is just too enticing. They may feel that they have to cheat and cut corners to give themselves an even chance in competing with people who start out with an advantage.

When A. Bartlett Giamatti was commissioner of major-league baseball, he had to deal with a pitcher, Kevin Gross, who had been caught cheating, scuffing a ball to make it easier to throw in a way that was harder to hit. Gross was a pitcher of average skill (for a professional athlete) and may have felt that he needed an edge to compete against major-league batters more talented than he. In handing down a fine and suspending the offending pitcher, Giamatti wrote: "Unlike acts of impulse or violence intended at the moment to vent frustration, acts of cheating are intended to alter the very conditions of play to favor one person. They seek to undermine the basic foundation of any contest, that all participants play under identical rules. They destroy faith in the games' integrity and fairness."

Sometimes people who have done something wrong are so ashamed of it that they follow up with another bad deed to keep the first misstep from being discovered. Unfaithful spouses spin a tangled web of lies to cover their affairs. Workers blame co-workers for their own mistakes. Public-school administrators have found that, incredible as it may seem, a certain number of parents will put their children's health at risk rather than face the embarrassment of admitting that they never had them vaccinated.

Sometimes people do wrong things out of anger. They may feel that life, or society, is unfair to them, so why should they have to be fair to society? They may not know what to do with their anger except to turn it on others. At its most extreme, there is the man who is fired, goes home to get a gun, and returns to shoot the boss who fired him and anyone else who gets in the way. At a less drastic, more generally recognizable level: You may have had a really bad day at work. Your boss criticized you, or a project you had worked on for weeks fell apart and had to be abandoned. There has been talk of downsizing, and you are afraid you may lose your job. You come home in a foul mood and yell at your children. They run to their rooms crying, believing it is their fault that you are upset. You feel terrible about making them feel that way, but you are too depressed to apologize and explain things to them.

I suspect we can all remember words we spoke or things we did when we were angry that we felt justified in doing at the time and now wish we could take back, or we at least wish we could convince people that those words and deeds don't accurately reflect the kind of people we are.

There is an event in the life of King David, told in chapter 6 of the second book of Samuel. It is the proudest day of David's life. He has captured the city of Jerusalem, made it his capital, and is now bringing the Ark of the Covenant into the city, to make Jerusalem Israel's religious as well as political center. When the Ark is carried into the city, it is accompanied by much singing and dancing, in which David exuberantly joins. David's wife, Michal, daughter of his predecessor King Saul, is offended by David's enthusiastic dancing, perhaps because she was raised with the dignity of a princess, perhaps because she feels left out of the celebration. She criticizes David for behaving in public like a common person instead of like a king. David is deeply hurt by her disapproval, which spoils his festive mood, and he strikes back at her where she is most vulnerable, saying, "I was dancing before the Lord *who chose me to be king instead of your father.*" The chapter concludes with these poignant words: "Michal the daughter of Saul had no child to the day of her death." Here were two people who had once loved each other deeply, but two moments of angry words, words they undoubtedly felt they needed to say and were justified in saying, destroyed that love.

So—are people basically good except when desperation, fear, or anger drive them to override the voice of conscience and do things they don't believe in? Some philosophers believe that people are born pure and innocent, and only when they discover that there aren't enough of the good things in life to satisfy everyone do they learn to compete, even connive, to get their share. Jean-Jacques Rousseau, the eighteenth-century French philosopher, wrote, "God makes all things good, then Man meddles with them and they become evil." Or are people basically mean and selfish, waiting only for the opportunity to get away with wickedness or for someone to give them permission to cast off the restraints of decency? Young children may look pure and innocent, but put two of them in a room with only a few toys and you will see where the propensity for future wars comes from. William Golding's novel *Lord of the Flies* tells of a group of boys stranded on a desert island with no adults around. In short order, they create a society as sadistic and destructive as any on earth. (In fairness, it should be pointed out that these youngsters were not randomly selected; they were stranded when a plane crashed that was evacuating them from a country at war.)

An experiment conducted some years ago by a psychologist at Yale, Dr. Stanley Milgram, raised some troubling implications regarding the human propensity for wrongdoing. Milgram told each subject that he or she was assisting in an important experiment in pain tolerance. A person whom he or she did not know was strapped into a chair and hooked up to an electric current. The subject was told that, by manipulating a lever, he could control the amount of electric shock the man in the chair would receive. He was also told that he could stop administering the electricity at any point for any reason, with no negative consequences. Actually, the man in the chair was an actor, the people at the switch were the real subjects of the experiment, and there was no electric shock.

The experiment began. At Milgram's command, each of the subjects "increased" the level of the electric jolt until the "patient" in the chair began to scream. The psychologist would say to the subject, "We're doing very well. This is important. Give him just a little more current." The patient/actor would cry out, "Please stop. For God's sake, stop! I can't take this!" But the subject would be told to ignore his cries and increase the voltage. Though the subjects had no reason to hurt the man in the chair, and though it had been emphasized to them that they could stop at any time, hardly anyone did. The subjects continued to apply what they believed to be painful torture to a total stranger because someone in authority told them to.

Milgram's conclusion: Now we can understand why, in the Second World War, "good Germans," men who were loving husbands and fathers and regular churchgoers, might have done such terrible things to their victims. To understand, I should point out, is not to excuse or justify. Courts have consistently rejected the defense "I was only following orders." Certainly the thousands of Germans who risked their lives and the safety of their families to save Jews during the Hitler years demonstrate that it was possible to follow one's conscience and refuse to go along with Nazi directives. But were the Germans who did join in the Nazi effort evil people following evil leaders, or were they just weak, intimidated, obedient people following evil leaders? Milgram suggests that people who have been taught to trust and support authority will defer to it even when that authority tells them to do something they find morally troubling. We seem to be able to say to ourselves, It doesn't seem right to me, but I'm sure he knows what he's doing, and if it's wrong, it will be his fault for telling me to do it.

Or perhaps Milgram's subjects went along with the experiment because there is a part of us that enjoys exercising power over others. There is a theory held by some criminologists, a theory I find plausible and will discuss at length in the next chapter, that many crimes are really about asserting power. These experts believe that the rapist is not looking for sex and the mugger is not looking for money as much as they are looking for the thrill of exercising power over another person. I can believe that this is especially tempting for people who worry about being taken seriously, people who may be insecure about their importance in the grand scheme of things and give in to the urge to demonstrate their ability to make a difference. One man imprisoned for brutally beating up his victim was quoted as saying, "I didn't care if I killed the guy or not. I just wanted to be his God for a little while." Maybe I could have told the couple in my study and my friend at the restaurant that sometimes people hurt and cheat each other to feel powerful, to cure their fear of insignificance.

In Dostoyevsky's classic novel *Crime and Punishment,* the student Raskolnikov murders his elderly landlady not because she has offended him or because he wants anything of hers, but because he wants to know the godlike feeling of being the master of life and death. In a world that has made him feel powerless and insignificant in so many ways, he is desperate to know the taste of power over another person.

Even nonviolent crimes may have an element of power hunger to them. The scam artist or embezzler who cheats people through an elaborate scheme may crave the satisfaction of manipulating his gullible victims more than he enjoys the money he takes from them. How often have you read about some such scheme and thought to yourself, If a clever person like that applied his imagination to earning an honest living, he could do just as well and not have to worry about going to prison.

So what kind of people are we? Are we naturally good and pure until external circumstances compromise our goodness? Or are we naturally weak and deceitful, needing conscience or outside authority to keep us in line? My answer is that we are both. I see every human being as having good and bad tendencies, impulses to charity and impulses to selfishness, the desire to be truthful and the desire to lie. These tendencies are in constant tension within us, even as the Bible describes Jacob and Esau struggling in Rebecca's womb when she was pregnant with them, even as Jacob had to struggle with part of himself to become the person he wanted to be. That would explain why good people can be corrupted by the prospect of financial gain or led astray by anger, and why criminals can display affection and loyalty.

Recently, my wife and I saw the movie *A Simple Plan*.

It begins with a man remembering his father having said that all a person needs to be happy is a good marriage and a good job. The man has a good, though limiting, job, and a good marriage, and he is happy. But shortly thereafter, he and two friends discover the wreckage of a private plane in a nearby field, with a dead pilot and several million dollars in cash. They realize that they have come upon some sort of criminal enterprise and that no good person will be hurt if they keep the money. Somehow the "simple plan" of keeping the money leads to tension, dissension, and murder, and the young couple who thought they were happy at the outset are psychologically scarred and ruined at the end. Some viewers may see the story as a parable of Original Sin and the inevitable depravity of people given a chance to do wrong (every man has his price; the only honest man is the guy who thinks somebody is watching). I saw it as an illustration of the sad truth that even good people have their breaking point. Even honest people will be tempted by large sums of money, and even faithful husbands will yield to temptation and lust, but that is not because they are sinners. It is because they are human.

Further, I would insist that there is something incomplete about us without that vulnerability. Jacob has to remain Jacob in part, even after he becomes Israel. Struggling with the angel makes him a better person, but it doesn't make him an angel. The gravitational pull of his humanity keeps him bound to the earth.

Do you remember the story of Dr. Jekyll and Mr. Hyde? Even if you have never read Robert Louis Stevenson's short novel, you are probably familiar with the plot. Henry Jekyll is a distinguished London physician, socially prominent and much loved by his friends. Because he is a good person (after all, he became a doctor in order to help people), he is troubled by the angry, aggressive feelings that occasionally well up inside him. Where do they come from? he wonders. Are they part of him, compromising his sense of himself as a man of exemplary character? Or are they a foreign element within him, like a malignant tumor that can be cut out or an infection that can be neutralized? Because he is a skilled chemist, he concocts a formula that will isolate the impulse to evil within him, hoping to find a way to banish it and ultimately change all humanity for the better. He drinks it and turns into someone else, a being he names Edward Hyde. Hyde is ugly in appearance and uglier in his soul. He is the embodiment of pure evil. Jekyll has succeeded in splitting himself into two people, one completely good, the other totally and unrelievedly evil. Hyde frightens people, runs over a little girl, and beats a man to death for a trivial slight. Jekyll has to swallow a second dose of the potion to become himself again. To his chagrin, he realizes that, for the time he lived as Hyde, he *enjoyed* being wicked. He enjoyed letting his aggression run free, unimpeded by conscience, much as Milgram's experimental subjects and tens of thousands of Nazi collaborators may at some level have enjoyed the permission to be cruel and dominating. He finds himself looking forward to becoming Hyde again, much as a drug addict finds himself craving his next fix. To Jekyll's still greater horror, he soon finds that he is turning into Hyde even without drinking the potion, and that the concoction is losing its power to turn him back; he has to take a double or triple dose. His only escape from this descent into depravity is to bring about his own death.

Published in 1886, this is one in a long line of cautionary tales warning us about the consequences when arrogant human beings, especially scientists, overreach themselves, using their intelligence to interfere with the kind of world God intended us to live in, a list that includes Mary Shelley's *Frankenstein* (1818) and Michael Crichton's *Jurassic Park*. But I find in the tale of Jekyll and Hyde another, perhaps more compelling, message. Stevenson's story says to me that the evil impulse is such an intimate part of every one of us that we cannot remove it, we cannot isolate it without drastically harming ourselves in the process. It would be like asking a brain surgeon to operate on us and remove the parts of our brains that give rise to "bad thoughts" without harming the rest.

A two-thousand-year-old Jewish fable makes a similar point in a more whimsical way, without Stevenson's brooding sense of tragedy. The traditional Jewish view of the human being sees God as planting in each of us something called the *yetzer ha-ra,* commonly translated as "the evil impulse" or "the will to do evil." I am inclined to translate it as "the will to selfishness" or "the egotistical principle." Just as doing mean or selfish things does not define us as evil people, the impulse that drives us to do mean or selfish things is not an "evil impulse." It is part of our humanity, the part that makes selfishness possible but not inevitable. The effort to be a good person is often pictured as a struggle to dominate the *yetzer ha-ra.*

The legend has it that one day people captured the *yetzer ha-ra* and locked it up. They celebrated their achievement, saying, "From now on, life will be Paradise. No evil, no lying or stealing." The next day, nobody opened his store for business, no one went courting or got married, and no babies were conceived. The people were embarrassed to realize that so many of the activities that were part of their normal lives, activities they enjoyed, honored, and depended on, contain an element of selfishness and aggression. Storekeepers and businesspeople try to outdo their competitors as fervently as professional athletes do, and society is often better off for the competition. Men and women marry not only for love but also in an effort to win for themselves the mates who will validate their attractiveness, the mates whom other people want. Without a modicum of selfishness and aggression, the world could not go on. It is a part of us, a problematic but essential part of us. So, reluctantly, they released the *yetzer ha-ra* from its captivity and resumed their daily struggle with it.

Some years ago, an episode of the television series *Star Trek* made a similar point. Captain Kirk, the commander of the spaceship *Enterprise,* was split into two Kirks, one totally good and moral, without an evil thought, and the other mean, selfish, and scheming. The point of the episode was that the good Kirk was totally ineffective, wanting to make good things happen but not able to. He had to be reunited with his worse half to become an effective leader again.

I believe that you can't be a complete person without having to wrestle with your own demons—and, for that matter, with your own angel. Like the man or woman who lifts weights at the gym to become stronger, a process known as "resistance training," we strengthen our moral fiber by the exercise of resisting temptation. Author and journalist David Denby has written, "You must be tempted or you cannot be good." I want to believe that about myself, because I know all too well the impulses that summon me to be selfish, impatient, insensitive. And I want to believe it about other people. I want to see them in the fullness of their humanity, to admire them for their goodness even as I become aware of the sordidness of which they are capable.

An example: We have learned that Martin Luther King, Jr., indulged in many extramarital dalliances while he was leading the battle for civil rights in the 1960s. That behavior does not diminish what King did to cleanse this nation's soul of the taint of racial segregation. I don't want to have to dismiss the civil-rights crusade because its leading exponent was guilty of adultery. I want to be able to admire the many things that Presidents Franklin Roosevelt, John Kennedy, and Bill Clinton did for this country despite what we have learned about their extramarital involvements. But at the same time, I don't want to say, Adultery can't be that bad if good people like Kennedy and King did it. What I end up saying is, Good people do bad things. If they weren't mightily tempted by their *yetzer ha-ra,* they might not be capable of the mightily good things they do. If they did not have to struggle with their less admirable impulses, they would not be complete people. If we could amputate the part of a person that leads him or her to be selfish and aggressive—if Dr. Jekyll had been successful in his well-intentioned experiment—it would be a disaster. What we'd be left with would be less than a whole human being.

Someone once said that the measure of a person's moral seriousness is what that person would do if he were sure nobody could see him. In one of the early sections of Plato's *Republic,* Socrates recounts the myth of the Ring of Gyges, a magic ring that has the power to make its wearer invisible. He asks how would an honest man behave if he were to wear it, or a dishonest man. Socrates' conclusion: If a person truly understood his own self-interest, he would not take advantage of his invisibility to do anything wrong. There would be nothing he could gain that would be worth the loss of his integrity, his right to think of himself as a good person.

Of course, there is no Ring of Gyges, but occasionally

real life imitates myth. A few years ago, there was a major power failure in parts of New York City. Streetlights, traffic lights, elevators, and burglar alarms stopped working. Some responded to the crisis by grabbing flashlights and helping people across streets and up darkened stairways. Others reacted by breaking store windows and helping themselves to the merchandise. We learned a lot about human nature that night, though nothing we learned should have surprised us. Sometimes the angel of conscience wins out over temptation; sometimes temptation gets the better of the angel.

Back when one of my congregational responsibilities was teaching the teenage confirmation class, I would put this puzzle to my students: Your business includes a string of coin-operated newspaper-vending machines. People deposit fifty cents, open the door, and take a paper. The problem is, once the door is open there is nothing to stop a person from taking more than one newspaper, significantly cutting into your profits. You decide to put a sign on the machine to keep people from doing that, and you are offered three suggestions as to what that sign should read:

A. This machine is under surveillance. If you take more than one newspaper, you will be subject to arrest. Stealing is against the law.

B. I depend on the income from this machine to support my family. Please don't steal from me.

C. Please don't take anything you haven't paid for. What kind of person are you?

In those three alternatives, you may recognize psychologist Lawrence Kohlberg's three stages of moral development: doing right out of fear of punishment, doing right out of a feeling of communal solidarity with others, and doing right because it is right.

For several years, I asked my teenage students two questions: Which of those three signs would be the most effective deterrent for most people? And which of them would be most effective for you personally? The results were consistent. The students unanimously rejected (A), arguing that the prospect of being arrested for stealing a newspaper was too remote to deter people. They chose (B) when it came to other people, but they chose (C) as most likely to influence their own behavior. They believed that they were basically good people (or perhaps they wanted me to believe that they were) and believed that others could be persuaded to do what was right by an appeal to sympathy, putting themselves in the vending machine owner's place.

Like most teenagers, they were idealistic. They wanted to believe in the goodness of the world, that people would do the right thing if we could just find the right words to persuade them. But at the same time, like most adolescents, they spent a lot of time contemplating with much discomfort their own readiness to lie, to exploit, to be cruel to the vulnerable. I suspect that is why the question "What kind of person are you?" resonated with them, even as it did for Jacob when, in the midst of his struggle, the angel asked him, "What is your name?" Who are you really? It is something those adolescents probably asked themselves twenty times a day.

Do we ever outgrow that adolescent tension, conscious of our commitment to what is right, yet conscious too of our vulnerability to doing what we know is not right? David Denby went back to his alma mater, Columbia University, thirty years after his graduation so that he could enroll as an adult in the freshman Humanities course he had taken as an eighteen-year-old. He describes his experience in his memoir *Great Books.* It was he who reintroduced me to the myth of the Ring of Gyges, the ring of invisibility. Pondering what he would do if he had such a ring, if he could go anywhere, do anything, and not be apprehended, Denby cannot think of anything that would be worth it, not if he had to live with the bitter aftertaste of the memory of having violated what he was about as a person. No act of revenge or financial gain would be worth it.

I recently ran across a story about a Native American tribal leader describing his own inner struggles. He said, "There are two dogs inside me. One of the dogs is mean and evil. The other dog is good. The mean dog fights the good dog all the time." Someone asked him which dog usually wins, and after a moment's reflection, he answered, "The one I feed the most."

Good people will do good things, lots of them, because they are good people. They will do bad things because they are human. In the daily, if not hourly, wrestling matches that set the tone of our lives, sometimes the angel wins and sometimes the angel loses. With luck, we will not be overwhelmed by guilt when the egotistical impulse defeats the angel, and we will understand that the victory is temporary, not permanent, when the angel wins. We will understand that, to be human, we need them both. But we will never stop asking ourselves, What kind of person do I want to be?

CHAPTER 4

Wild Justice: The Seductive Pleasure of Getting Even

Sometimes the problem we face in our struggle to be good people is not so much a matter of doing what is right as of choosing between two rights. A professor of mine at seminary used to say, "The hardest choices you and the people you counsel will have to make will not be between good and evil, but between good and good. You will find yourselves able to do something you feel is right and good only by sacrificing an equally good and right goal." It is not only a matter of time pressure: If you give blood or serve on the local school board, that's time you can't spend with your family. It is something that happens when two values we believe in come into conflict and we have to deny one to affirm the other.

We face this dilemma, for example, when someone hurts us. Part of us wants to pay the person back, to get even, to give him what he deserves, while another part of us is uncomfortable at the prospect of having to lower ourselves to his level in order to get even. We feel justified, even righteous, in getting back at someone who has done us wrong, but at the same time we feel more than a little bit morally compromised.

The fact that so many great plays and novels (*Hamlet,* the Greek tragedies of Aeschylus, *The Count of Monte Cristo*) have the theme of revenge at their core, and that popular novels and movies about revenge have the ability to grab us emotionally, should tell us how deeply we feel on the subject. I have heard movie audiences cheer when the fictional hero finally catches up with the fictional villain, so emotionally involved are they in the story. Revenge, and fantasies of revenge, are among the strongest emotions we feel. They are nearly universal, nearly irresistible, and often deeply troubling.

The title of this chapter is taken from a remark by the sixteenth-century English writer Francis Bacon: "Revenge is a kind of wild justice, which the more men's nature runs to, the more ought law to weed it out." In that one sentence, Bacon tells us four important things about revenge:

- It is something that a lot of people are drawn to.
- It is natural, instinctive, not something we have to learn.
- It resembles justice but is unlike justice in important ways.
- It is undesirable. It is natural the way weeds are natural,

and, if not checked, it will crowd out healthier emotions even as weeds choke off the more desirable cultivated plants.

I define revenge as punishment in the name of justice, tarnished by taking pleasure in hurting the person being punished. And therein lies the problem. We want to punish wrongdoers because we want to live in a safe and just world, a world in which people are protected from criminals and wrongdoers suffer the consequences of their bad behavior. If we can't count on nature to protect good people (germs affect them as they affect everyone), and if we can't count on human nature to protect good people (murderers and robbers prey on the vulnerable), can we at least count on society to protect good people by imposing fines and prison terms on those who would harm us? Or do we have to take justice into our own hands?

But if we believe in meting out justice, we also need to believe that we are good people, and part of us feels guilty when we have hurt someone, even if we believe that person deserves to be hurt. We are uncomfortable *enjoying* the thought of hurting another person. This is another instance of our wanting to be good people but finding ourselves doing things, or fantasizing about doing things, that a good person would not do. A statement by the World Council of Churches condemns revenge as an attempt not to *transcend* suffering but to *extend* it, to make someone else hurt as we have been hurt. Does the world really become a better place, they ask, if we hurt someone for having hurt us?

We have all heard the adage "Revenge is sweet." But did you know that that familiar saying is really a corruption and misinterpretation of the original wording? Milton, in *Paradise Lost,* wrote, "Revenge, at first though sweet, bitter ere long upon itself recoils." In other words, as Milton knew and as many of us painfully discover, revenge is sweet in the contemplation but bitter in the carrying out. The target of our revenge deserves to be hurt, and part of us is eager to hurt him because of what he did to us, but another part of us feels diminished by doing the hurting. As Shakespeare has Hamlet say in what is probably the greatest revenge drama ever written, "The time is out of joint; O cursed spite, / That ever I was born to set it right."

Freud believed that Hamlet could not bring himself to kill the man who had murdered his father and married his mother because Hamlet himself had unconsciously wished to do those things. But isn't it equally possible that Hamlet could not do it because he did not want to be a murderer? When, in the last act, he finally does expose and kill his father's killer, he too dies, perhaps as Shakespeare's way of telling us that Hamlet was destroyed morally as well as physically by his all-consuming quest for vengeance.

The ambivalence in getting even is that our consciences condemn it even as our souls crave it. It has been suggested that Shakespeare set his great revenge plays, *Hamlet, Othello,* and *Coriolanus,* not in England but in Denmark, Cyprus, and Rome as a way of playing to his audience's emotions, giving them what they wanted to see, while at the same time saying, These people doing these things are not us. They are exotic foreigners.

I can appreciate that ambivalence. I have sat in movie theatres, my heart rejoicing at the retributive violence of Clint Eastwood's Dirty Harry Callahan even as my head was condemning the mindless destruction. And a passage in the Talmud describes God as rebuking the angels who were cheering at the sight of the Egyptian army drowning in the Red Sea: "How can you cheer? They too are My creatures." If even angels are moved to delight at the downfall of the wicked, how can we not be? And if God condemns the angels' delight as improper, how can we not be embarrassed by our own?

That moment when the community as a whole claimed for itself the right and responsibility to punish criminals, taking the role away from the injured parties, represents one of the great advances in the history of civilization. Punishment could now be administered coolly, objectively, by an outsider who would feel no vindictiveness and take no personal pleasure in its administration. It would be justice without vengeance. Susan Jacoby, in her history of revenge, *Wild Justice,* writes, "One measure of a civilization's complexity is the distance between the aggrieved individual and the administration of justice." Problems arise, however, when people fear that they cannot depend on society to administer justice, that the courts are slow, unreliable, or inclined to play favorites, or that the law is full of loopholes that let the guilty escape. We then face the uncomfortable choice between letting a guilty person go free and taking the responsibility for punishing into our own hands, with the bitter aftertaste and sense of moral compromise that often entails.

Once, in an age of religious faith, people believed they could depend on God to punish the criminal who cheated justice in court. The Talmud describes an incident in which the head of the Israelite Supreme Court saw a man with a knife chasing another man into a cave. He heard a scream and saw the pursuer come out of the cave with his knife dripping blood. The man laughed at the rabbi, saying, You probably believe I did something terrible, but the evidence is all circumstantial, and, besides, there is no second witness, as the law requires. There is nothing you can do to me. As the Talmud tells it, before the man had taken ten steps, a snake bit him and he died.

But in our secular age, that gap between crime and punishment can lead to vigilantism and mob justice, as frustrated people take the law into their own hands. Or it can give rise to the emergence of outlaws in the Robin Hood tradition, for whom Americans have always felt a certain irrational admiration, men denied justice who feel morally superior to the society that has mistreated them. I have heard movie audiences cheer Charles Bronson in the *Death Wish* series. I have listened countless times to Joan Baez singing the praises of Pretty Boy Floyd, the outlaw victimized by a corrupt sheriff, who robbed banks and used the money (at least in the song and legend) to help the poor. I have identified emotionally with Coalhouse Walker, the young black man in the novel, movie, and musical *Ragtime* who embarked on a pattern of destructiveness when the authorities ignored what had been done to him, even as I told myself that what he did was unjustified. And I remember fondly, if sadly, the ending of my all-time favorite Western movie, *Shane,* where Alan Ladd, having gunned down a vicious killer and his corrupt employer, rides away from the town he has saved. He has to leave, not because his work is done, but because he has shed blood in an act of vengeance. His tarnished presence would contaminate the community that has been restored to a peaceful paradise, a community in which a man of the gun like him has no place. (Is the name Shane a play on Cain, who was condemned to wander the earth forever because he had shed blood?)

And, of course, access to the courts, however reliable, does not apply to the petty offenses that don't justify calling in the authorities but stimulate the thirst for revenge just the same: the person who is mean to our child, the neighbor whose dog barks all night, the man or woman who lies to us or lies to others about us.

What are we to do with this troubling emotion, the desire to get even? Most of the time when there is a conflict between impulse and conscience, we know that the right answer is to follow our conscience, even if we are not always strong enough to do it. But what do we do when revenge appeals to us in the noble name of justice, asking us to make the world a better place by giving someone what he or she deserves?

Some voices, in the name of religion or in the name of a more compassionate society, would urge us to forgive as the only way to break the cycle of hatred and violence. For Christians, the obligation to forgive as they hope to be forgiven is included in the Lord's Prayer and incorporated in Jesus' admonition to turn the other cheek. Jews are told in the Torah, "You shall not hate your brother in your heart," and the great commandment in Leviticus 19:18, "You shall love your neighbor as yourself," is preceded by the words "You shall not take revenge or bear a grudge." (A commentator on the Jewish legal code defines taking revenge as saying, "I won't lend you my garden hose, because when you borrowed my shovel you broke it." Bearing a grudge is saying, "I'll lend you my garden hose, even though when you borrowed my shovel you broke it." The attitude we should strive for is to say, "I'll lend you my garden hose because you're my neighbor.")

It is cleansing to be able to forgive, to rid your soul of the bitterness that is an inevitable ingredient of plotting revenge against the person who has hurt you. If we fantasize about getting even and never act on it, which is what most of us do, we end up embittering ourselves and not affecting the other person at all. I remember telling a divorcée who was still angry at her ex-husband for having left her ten years earlier, "Look at what you've been doing all these years. You've been standing here in Massachusetts holding a hot coal in your hand, waiting for your ex-husband to walk by so you can throw it at him. Meanwhile, he has been living happily in New Jersey with his new family, and you've burned your hand waiting." And when we act on our vengeful schemes, we too often feel that we have diminished ourselves, that we have lowered ourselves to the level of our adversary. We think less of ourselves, and we fear that others will think less of us. The prospect of getting even is seldom worth what it does to us as people. It has been said that we should try to rise above the wish for revenge, not to be saintly but to be sensible. Life is too precious to be wasted on hatred. But we all know how hard it is to follow that advice.

Several years ago, because my previous book dealt with the issue of forgiveness, I was invited to appear on a daytime talk show on that subject. The first forty-five minutes of the show consisted of interviews with people to whom terrible things had been done and who had gone out of their way to forgive those who had hurt them. There was a woman whose father, a minister in a high-crime area, had been killed by a man who also shot her and left her crippled. There was a man who, as a child, had been abducted, badly injured, and left to die by a man his father had fired. As the show unfolded, I could sense the discomfort of the audience: Why are these people so different from me? I can't forgive the person who dented my car in the parking lot, and they visited their assailants in prison to forgive them! The moderator of the show challenged them: If you're looking for people to visit to make them feel better, why don't you visit sick children in hospitals rather than criminals who treated you so badly? When I came on at the end of the show, as the "expert" on the spiritual process that enables people to forgive, I suggested that these people were not saints. They were not that different from the rest of us. They needed to confront and forgive those who had hurt them as a way of achieving closure, convincing themselves that these people were not worth being obsessed with. One of them told me before the show, "If I continued to hate that man, I would be giving him more power over me than he deserves. Forgiving him was a way of banishing him from my soul." Similarly, I read what a Bosnian woman who had been raped and tortured in Serbia told a reporter: "To seek revenge, you have to hate. But how can you hate someone so repulsive? He is not worth my hating."

What can we do about this dilemma, when we feel part of our souls strongly drawn toward dreams of getting even while part of us reluctantly recognizes that such dreams are unworthy of us?

First, we have to separate judicial punishment from the issues of forgiving or seeking vengeance. We don't have to hate the mugger, the drunk driver, the dishonest salesman who cheated us, if we can count on the police to apprehend them, the courts to try them, and juries to convict them. We don't have to waste our energy and coarsen our souls with daydreams of revenge. We can even try to understand what would drive a person to commit a crime or to drink and drive without feeling that we were relieving those who injured us of responsibility for what they did. Remember Susan Jacoby's remark about measuring the maturity of a civilization by the distance it creates between the victim and the administration of justice. The legal system has the responsibility of deciding whether or not a person deserves to be punished, and if so, how seriously. It can proclaim "guilty" or "not guilty," *but it has no right to forgive.* Aryeh Neier, former executive director of the American Civil Liberties Union, has written, "Public forgiveness and private vengeance both depreciate the victim. Respect for those who suffer requires that no one usurp the victim's exclusive right to forgive. It similarly requires that the duty to punish be assumed by everyone other than the victim."

I am bothered by the readiness of some people to forgive injuries done to someone else. Uninjured themselves, they either tell us that crime is society's fault and the wrongdoer is as much a victim as we are, or assure us that God has forgiven the criminal as God forgives us all for our sins. I reject that view. I am in favor of tracking down eighty-five-year-old ex-Nazis and making them stand trial for their war crimes, not because I am a vindictive person—I have no desire to hurt them myself—but because I pay them the compliment of seeing them as human beings who are responsible for the consequences of their behavior, and because I believe, with Hamlet, that "the time is out of joint" as long as serious crimes go unpunished. For the same reason, I was very disappointed some years ago to read the newspaper account of a deeply religious woman, the victim of a brutal assault, who refused to testify against her attacker, claiming that on religious grounds she had forgiven him and had no desire for revenge. To me, that seemed to be an inappropriate violation of the separation of church and state. As an individual, the woman had every right to forgo the desire to get even, and I admire her for it. But as a citizen, she should have felt the obligation to ensure the safety of her neighbors by helping to get a dangerous man off the streets.

But there is something else, something more radical, that we can do to wean ourselves from our troubling attraction to getting even. If criminologists are correct in believing that much crime is really about exercising power over another person, as I suggested previously, then perhaps the instinctive desire for revenge is less about hurting the person who has hurt us and more about restoring the power balance to what it was before the crime. We don't really want to hurt our assailant so much as we want to reclaim from him the power, the sense of being in control of our lives, that he stole from us. We don't really want to break the windows of the neighbor who owns the barking dog. We just want to stop feeling helpless, and if we could find a more honorable way of doing that, we would choose it.

Consider what has happened in South Africa after the end of apartheid. Faced with thousands of acts of murder and brutality committed by hundreds of soldiers, police, and other government officials over the course of decades, the new government realized that trying to bring every guilty party to trial would tie up the courts for years, rekindle bitter feelings, and racially divide a country that desperately needed to heal. What they did instead was to establish the Truth and Reconciliation Commission, whose purpose was partly to get the perpetrators to confess their crimes and show remorse under a promise of amnesty, but mostly to serve as a forum for victims to tell their stories in public and be listened to. I suspect that even those who created the Truth and Reconciliation Commission could not have foreseen how great the healing power of being listened to and taken seriously would turn out to be. A man who had been blinded by the police during a brutal interrogation said after testifying, "I feel that what had been making me sick all these years was the fact that I could not tell my story. But now, it feels like I got my sight back." The mother of a young man killed by the police told an interviewer, "If this means that this perpetrator, the man who killed my son, becomes human again, so that I and all of us get our humanity back, then I agree, I support it."

These victims and relatives of victims, good, decent people, did not want to hurt those who had hurt them, though they may have thought they did. They wanted their dignity as human beings restored to them, and when the commission endorsed their testimony, they got their dignity back. They wanted to reclaim power over their own lives, and seeing their torturers contrite, humiliated before the commission, gave them that. Some felt unsatisfied that so many wrong-doers were not punished more severely; most, however, felt no need to see them hurt. The commission had given them what they needed. Revenge would have been an inadequate substitute.

This healing was an unanticipated outcome, but perhaps it should not have been a total surprise. Similar investigations took place in Argentina and Chile, though less systemati-cally, when democratic governments replaced brutal military dictatorships. Soldiers and policemen confessed to acts of torture and murder. They wept on the witness stand and expressed remorse. In most cases, the victims and their fami-lies felt no need to divide their anguished country again by demanding further punishment. In Ariel Dorfman's play *Death and the Maiden,* a Chilean woman identifies the doctor who raped and tortured her as an agent of the repressive gov-ernment. She takes him captive and is about to kill him, even as he insists on his innocence. But when he breaks down and confesses his guilt and admits how ashamed he is for what he did, she has no need to punish him further. His humiliation has done more to heal her than his death could have.

Stories came out of Europe after the Second World War of

Holocaust survivors who had spent years dreaming of taking revenge on their captors if they survived and then rejected that revenge when they saw their tormentors stripped of power and left vulnerable. One man said he realized he would become like them if he let himself do what he was tempted to do once he had them in his power.

One word in an article about South Africa's Truth and Reconciliation Commission caught my attention. Psychologist Judith Herman, in the magazine *The American Prospect,* wrote, "What victims most commonly seek is vindication. They want public acknowledgment that what happened to them was wrong. They want the burden of shame lifted from their shoulders and placed where it belongs."

Shame? Why should the victims feel ashamed? The robber, the rapist, the torturer is the one who has reason to feel ashamed. Over the years, I have counseled rape victims and incest survivors, and I have always been puzzled by the feeling of shame I encountered in them. What did they have to be ashamed of? They were innocent victims! Only recently did I come to understand them. The shame they felt was the shame of powerlessness, the inability to protect the integrity of their own bodies. People have described to me what it felt like to be mugged. I have spoken to Holocaust survivors about their experiences, including a man who saw his parents taken away to be killed when he was six years old. What they all remember most vividly is not the cruelty of their tormentors but their own feelings of helplessness.

I learned a great truth from them. When we thirst for revenge, it isn't really revenge we are after. We are looking to reclaim the sense of power and dignity that was stolen from us. If there were a less morally tainted way of feeling empowered when we confront our adversary, if we could claim power over him without having to hurt him, most of us would be satisfied with that.

Some years ago, the American legal system created what is known as the Victim Impact Statement. After a defendant has been found guilty but before sentencing, the victim's relatives are invited to tell the court what the crime—the murder, the robbery, the drunk-driving death—has done to their family. They speak about what a wonderful person the victim was and how their lives will never be the same, how an adolescent girl will have to grow up without the father she idolized, how parents had to bury their only child. The intended purpose was to assist judges and juries in matching the severity of the sentence to the impact of the crime on people's lives. But, as in South Africa, there was another, unintended consequence. In about half the cases where family members are invited to give a statement, once they have been listened to it no longer matters to them how severe the sentence is. They want the criminal off the streets and in jail to protect others, but they no longer need to see him suffer. The experience of being listened to and taken seriously by the judge and jury cured that feeling of helplessness that being a victim imposed on them, and restored their power.

The advance of civilization may require detaching the victim from the judicial and punitive process, but doing so creates an emotional void in the victim's soul. People cry out, I'm the one who was raped! It was my child who was killed! Why is the trial "the state versus . . ." and I'm left out? Inviting the victim to speak and taking his or her words seriously helps to fill that void.

I have recently become aware of a trend in American legal circles known as Restorative Justice. Whereas the aim of retributive justice is to determine the right punishment, supporters of Restorative Justice explain themselves this way: "The first priority is to work toward the healing and restoration of the victim. The second priority is to hold the offender accountable for his actions, involving the offender in the decision as to how to make things right for the victim and for the community, which has also been harmed, with the goal of re-integrating both the victim and the offender back into the community. . . . Restorative Justice redefines justice in a way that looks to the future rather than the past." Restorative Justice sees the courtroom drama as a dialogue between the victim and the community, rather than a duel between the prosecutor and the defense attorney. The victim gets to tell her story without being cross-examined by a lawyer with an interest in challenging her testimony. It turns out that most victims don't necessarily want to see anyone punished. We recall Judith Herman's words, "They want public acknowledgment that what happened to them was wrong." An incest survivor I have counseled told me that she has gone through years of therapy and support groups but still does not feel whole because she has never been able to get her brother to say, "You were innocent and I did a terribly wrong thing to you." That one sentence, she believes, would do more to heal her than anything else.

Events in South Africa and in American criminal courtrooms can help us understand that we don't have to hurt another person in order to claim the satisfaction that we think revenge will give us. If what we really crave is to regain a sense of being empowered, to be restored, there are other ways to do that, ways that will leave us feeling better about the kind of people we are. Depending on the circumstances, we can turn to the authorities for action or at least for validation of the justice of our cause. We can sit down in a nonconfrontational way with the friend or neighbor who has offended us, not to demand an apology but to tell him or her how we feel and why we are upset, focusing on our feelings rather than on his misbehavior. His reaction may surprise us. Sometimes (alas, not always) the offender will turn out to be responsive, not the demon our imaginations had imagined him to be. As an example of the *wrong* way to do this, I remember the member of my congregation whose recently married son was having problems with his new wife. The congregant told me about them and said, "I was thinking of going to talk to her mother about it." I said I thought that was a good idea, but the congregant went on to say, "I'm going to ask her why she raised her daughter to be such a self-ish person." As you might guess, the marriage did not last much longer.

I am often invited to speak to medical groups, to help them see medical care from the perspective of the patient and the patient's family. I tell them that a lot of malpractice suits are filed not because doctors make mistakes but because patients get the feeling (exacerbated by pressures of managed-care plans) that doctors don't care about them. I have heard of successful efforts to mediate patient complaints without going to court by bringing doctor and patient together to listen to each other's side of the story. Typically, the doctor will apologize for a lapse in good judgment and describe steps he is taking to ensure that it never happens again. The patient will admit that he or she had unrealistic expectations and was emotionally upset at the moment. Instead of an expensive and angry adversarial confrontation in court, we end up with two winners and no losers.

And if all else fails, we can choose to feel empowered by deciding to rise above the situation, whether serious or relatively trivial—not forgiving, not forgetting, but transcending. Someone once compared getting into an argument with a boorish neighbor to wrestling in the mud with a pig: You will both get filthy, but the pig will enjoy it. In any conflict, we have the option of walking away, not out of weakness or fear but out of strength, deciding that the price paid in gaining some satisfaction is more than we are willing to pay. I have often found myself asking people, "Are you strong enough to forgive? Or is the notion of getting even the only power you have over someone who has hurt you?" Forgiveness, I try to tell them, is a favor we do ourselves, not a favor we do the other party.

In the Bible, the book of Exodus describes the suffering of the Hebrew people as slaves in Egypt. Pharaoh, the Egyptian ruler, ordered that male children be drowned at birth. Hebrew slaves were set to work making bricks to build Pharaoh's palaces and storehouses, and were whipped if they did not meet their daily quota. When they complained, Pharaoh made them gather their own straw for brickmaking instead of supplying it. It took God's miraculous intervention to redeem them from their misery. That is why it is surprising to read in the book of Deuteronomy (23:7), "You shall not hate an Egyptian because you were strangers in his land." You shall not hate the Egyptians for having mistreated you so badly, not because they deserve your forgiveness but because you deserve better than to be permanently mired in the bitterness of the past. As long as your soul is corroded by hatred, you are still their slave. At the Passover Seder, when Jews celebrate the memory of the Exodus from Egypt, we taste a bitter herb before the meal to recall the bitterness of slavery, then immediately override the bitter taste with matzo and wine, symbols of liberation.

Once we recognize that the thirst for revenge is really a need to reclaim power, to shed the role of victim and substitute action for helplessness, we can find ways of meeting that need without hurting another person and compromising our own goodness. I came across a fascinating example of this in the memoirs of Nadezhda Mandelstam, a Russian poet and widow of an even more celebrated poet, Osip Mandelstam, who was arrested by Stalin's secret police in 1934 and died in prison shortly afterward. Some years later, his widow learned that a woman had betrayed him to the authorities, feeding them false information about his disloyalty to Stalin. That woman, a member of the Mandelstams' social circle, was a professional informer whose treachery had resulted in the imprisonment, torture, and death of several of their mutual friends. Nadezhda also learned that this woman would shortly be hosting an elaborate party to celebrate her fiftieth birthday, and crafted a plan of revenge. She gathered the survivors of all those whom the woman had betrayed and planned to crash the party, humiliating the woman in the presence of her closest friends. On the night of the party, this assemblage of the bereaved and betrayed rang the doorbell of the woman's apartment. The woman opened the door, saw them, and fainted. At that point, the unexpected happened. The people whose lives she had ruined picked her up, carried her to a sofa, brought her a glass of water, and revived her. When she had recovered, they left without saying another word. No exposure, no humiliation. Once they saw their betrayer vulnerable and helpless, the desire for revenge left them. They had no need to lower themselves to her level by hurting a helpless person. They had gotten what they needed.

Most of the time, our dilemmas about revenge are personal. We are tempted to get even with someone who has injured or offended us. But sometimes the collective feelings of two hundred million Americans on the issue of revenge coalesce into public policy. Government leaders take note of our opinions and, both because they want to be elected and because they feel obliged to represent our wishes, they translate our feelings into law. The most conspicuous example of this is the issue of capital punishment, executing people who have committed particularly horrifying crimes.

For as long as I can remember, I have been deeply ambivalent about capital punishment. One day I would be in favor of it yet feel embarrassed and morally compromised by favoring the deliberate taking of a human life. I would read the account of a particularly brutal, sadistic murder and find myself saying, "Anybody who would do that doesn't deserve to live. Execution by lethal injection is too good for him. He should be made to suffer before he dies, the way his victim did." When I saw the movie *Dead Man Walking,* which was supposed to move people to oppose capital punishment, I found myself taking satisfaction in the death of the killer of two innocent young people. In fact, I was outraged by the movie's concentration on the killer's situation, nearly ignoring the pain of the murdered girl's father, portraying him as a less-than-whole person for his inability to forgive.

But at other times, I would be against capital punishment, mindful of the danger that an innocent man could be executed because of overzealous prosecutors, incompetent defense, or the intimidating atmosphere of a public crying for blood. I would be bothered by the likelihood of a death sentence's being influenced by the race and social class of the victim, or the side of a state or county line on which a crime occurred.

And I was not alone in my ambivalence. When the Supreme Court narrowly upheld the constitutionality of capital punishment, the nine justices issued nine separate opinions, each having a different reason for accepting or denouncing it. One of the nine, writing for the majority, validated the deep emotional need of the public to exact the ultimate punishment for the ultimate crime as "neither forbidden nor inconsistent with our respect for the dignity of man."

But once we realize that there are other ways for survivors to reclaim the power over life and death that the murderer has wrongly appropriated than by killing the murderer, and once we come to understand that, like Shane, like Hamlet, we destroy a bit of our own humanity by giving in to the natural, instinctive desire to hurt as we have been hurt, then we will be able to find punishments short of execution but severe enough to match the severity of the crime. We can protect society without taking pleasure in the suffering of the criminal. A society that executes criminals is like a parent who hits his child because he is frustrated, because the child has mocked his claim of authority and he doesn't know any other way of making it clear that he is in charge. But at least the individual parent will usually feel bad about the spanking or beating. We don't have to kill criminals to reclaim power over them. Putting the murderer in prison for life, without possibility of parole, ensures us that he will never murder again, and this is as serious a punishment as we should want to inflict. All it lacks is the emotional satisfaction of taking a bad person's life, and even if we were completely confident that no innocent person would ever be executed, that satisfaction is one we are better off without. That the sadistic murderer deserves to suffer is beside the point; that we deserve better than to be the instrument of another human being's suffering is very much the point.

The Bible, in a series of events that take place toward the end of Jacob's life, gives us one of the great stories of revenge and the redemptive power of forgoing it. You may remember the story. Jacob's sons are murderously jealous of their young brother Joseph because he is their father's favorite. Joseph has fed their jealousy by telling them of a dream he had in which they would all bow down to him. They sell him as a slave to a passing caravan on its way to Egypt. There, by God's grace and a series of fortuitous events, Joseph becomes vice-regent of Egypt and is put in charge of distributing food during a long famine. The famine drives Joseph's brothers to come to

Egypt to beg the vice-regent to sell them grain. Joseph recognizes them, though they do not recognize him, and he realizes that this is his opportunity to get even with them for what they did to him, as he has dreamed of doing for twenty years. (Joseph had named his first son Manasseh, which means "forgetting," because God has helped him forget the misfortune that sent him into Egypt. The name is, of course, an admission that he has not forgotten at all, rather like sending a birthday card to the boyfriend or girlfriend who rejected you, telling him or her, "I just want you to know I'm not thinking about you.") He devises an elaborate scheme, which involves putting the money they paid for the grain back into their sacks, along with a golden cup of his own, so that he will have grounds to imprison them, making slaves of them as they made a slave of him. But when he sees them distraught and humbled, he can't go through with it. He realizes that he doesn't really want vengeance, he wants family; and he understands that if he punishes every person who does him wrong he will have satisfaction, he may even have justice, but he will have neither friends nor family. Like Shane, he will be left alone in his righteousness. Like Hamlet, he will have destroyed himself in the process of getting even. So he drops his disguise, bursts into tears, and reveals himself to his brothers, saying, "I am Joseph; is our father still alive?"

A few of us will be victims of serious crimes, and we can hope that society will administer swift and appropriate justice. All of us will be victims of cruelty, thoughtless behavior, and petty annoyances. At times like that, we will have to choose between the seductive appeal of getting even, attractive but harmful to our souls, and the cleansing force of integrity, reclaiming power over our lives precisely by not giving in to the temptation to get even. And we will know which side the angel is on.

CHAPTER 5

Shalom: The Quest for Integrity

On Monday night, December 11, 1995, a fire broke out in the factory complex of Malden Mills, a textile manufacturing plant in the industrial city of Lawrence, Massachusetts, some thirty miles from my home. By the time firefighters from Lawrence and several surrounding communities were able to bring it under control, most of the buildings were gone. Fortunately, no lives were lost, but the psychological and economic impact on the city of Lawrence was devastating. Malden Mills' three thousand employees faced the prospect of no jobs two weeks before Christmas. Almost everyone in Lawrence assumed that the mill's owner would take advantage of the opportunity to relocate his plant to a low-wage area in the South or overseas. They feared the city would lose its biggest economic asset.

It didn't happen. A day after the fire, Aaron Feuerstein, owner of Malden Mills and grandson of the company's founder, announced that all the people on his payroll would receive their salaries for the next three months though there would be no work for them to do, and that he would rebuild the plant on its site. He was quoted as saying, "I have a responsibility to the workers and an equal responsibility to the community. It would be unconscionable to put three thousand people on the streets and deliver a death blow to the city of Lawrence. Maybe on paper my company is worth less to Wall Street but I can tell you it is worth more."

Feuerstein became a national hero, the subject of laudatory stories on television and in magazines. President Clinton invited him as his guest to the State of the Union Address and introduced him, sitting next to Mrs. Clinton, to a national audience.

What makes a man like Feuerstein act so decently, putting the welfare of his workers and their community (he himself does not live in Lawrence) ahead of his own financial self-interest? Feuerstein is a devout Jew. He prays daily, and studies the Bible and Talmud regularly. But as we have seen, many devout adherents of their religions can be less than ideal neighbors and citizens. Feuerstein's faith has given him an additional quality, one that can be summed up in a word that was used repeatedly when the media told the Malden Mills story to an admiring nation: integrity.

Integrity means being whole, unbroken, undivided. It describes a person who has united the different parts of his or her personality, so that there is no longer a split in the soul.

When your soul is divided, part of you wants to do one thing while part wants to do something else: Do you tell the prospective buyer of your home about the plumbing problem or do you keep quiet unless he asks? Do you spend your money on a vacation or give it to charity? Do you resist temptation or give in? You are at war with yourself, and the struggle leaves you uncomfortable. When you have integrity, all of your aspirations are focused in one direction. Like the karate expert who can break a board with his bare hand by focusing all his strength on one spot, the person of integrity, the person whose soul is not fragmented, can do great things by concentrating all of his energies on a single goal. For the person of integrity, life may not be easy but it is simple: Figure out what is right and do it. All other considerations come in second.

During the 2000 presidential election, writer James Fallows posed the question: What makes an effective leader, whether in politics or business? What characterizes the man or woman whom others are eager to follow? His answer was "a sense of wholeness," the feeling that the person is all of one piece, that there is a consistency to him, that he will be the same person tomorrow that he is today and will apply the same value system to one question that he does to all questions. That is why we often find ourselves saying admiringly of a candidate with whose positions we strongly disagree, "At least you know where he stands." Just as adolescents who are insecure about their bodies excessively admire the attractive or athletically gifted classmate, adults who are uncomfortable with their own moral inconsistencies admire the person who seems to "have it together."

The familiar Hebrew word *shalom,* usually translated "peace," means more than the absence of quarreling. *Shalom* means wholeness, everything fitting together, nothing missing and nothing broken. Just as peace on the world scene means no fighting between nations, no quarreling with other people, *shalom* for you as an individual means no fighting with yourself, no quarreling between the two halves of your divided soul. To wish someone *shalom* is to wish him or her the blessing of wholeness and integrity.

Ten months after the Malden Mills fire, Bruce Butterfield of the *Boston Globe* looked back at what had been accomplished and wrote, "In the days and months since then, a third-generation mill owner driven by pride, religion and a sense of family would battle with insurance companies, government officials, competitors out to steal his customers, his own managers and even himself to do something nobody in modern times had attempted: rebuild a textile mill in an old New England mill city. . . . Months later, he and his mill remain a national media event: the story of a devout Jew whose generosity at Christmastime made him a Frank Capra–like hero in an era of corporate greed and downsizing."

Shortly after that story appeared, I met Aaron Feuerstein at a conference on spirituality in the workplace. He was the opening speaker and spoke very movingly. I was the closing speaker, and I had been so impressed with him that I departed from my prepared remarks to point out that, in German and Yiddish, the name Feuerstein means "fire stone." It originally must have referred to a flint, a stone you would use to start a fire. But I suggested we might interpret Feuerstein, the "firestone," as the stone that survived the fire. Because it had integrity, because it was whole and not broken, it did not burn. It was not destroyed by the fire when everything else was. Rather, it absorbed the heat of the fire and was able to provide warmth to others in the cold December days that followed.

Feuerstein is a special person, a man of integrity, but, fortunately, he is not unique among business leaders. I learned that from a conversation I had some years ago in Cleveland, where I had been part of a book-and-author event sponsored by the *Cleveland Plain Dealer*. One of my fellow panelists was Kenneth Blanchard, author of the *One Minute Manager* books, a best-selling series of slim volumes on effectiveness in business. After the program, we found ourselves waiting at adjoining gates at the airport, with nearly an hour until his plane would carry him back to California and mine would bring me home to Massachusetts. We got to talking, and I was very taken with Blanchard and with his goals for his books. He believes that God has put him on earth to humanize business relationships between employer and employee, between salesperson and customer. In today's workplace, so many of our interactions have become impersonal. We deal with strangers. We use people and discard them rather than see them as fellow human beings. Blanchard's books contain such bits of advice as reminders to managers to take time to compliment employees whenever appropriate, to "catch them doing something right" instead of speaking to them only when they have done something wrong. This is not simply a tactic for getting them to be more productive but part of an effort to make the office or factory a more humane place to work, a place where neither manager nor employee has to sacrifice his soul for the sake of the company. Blanchard warns managers that employees who feel they are ill-used and unappreciated as people will find ways to "get even" by taking excessive sick leave, pilfering company property, or giving less than their best effort at work.

Blanchard co-authored a book with the Reverend Norman Vincent Peale called *The Power of Ethical Management,* whose central message is summed up in one of its key sentences: "There is no right way to do a wrong thing." The book is a plea for integrity in the business world, both as a tactic (companies that encourage employees to lie and cheat to increase sales will find those employees padding their expense accounts and taking company secrets with them when they change jobs) and as a matter of principle (what does it profit a man if he wins a promotion but loses his soul in the process?). The authors urge their readers to ask themselves: "If we have to cheat to win, shouldn't we think twice about what business we're in?"

How do we become models of integrity like Aaron Feuerstein and Ken Blanchard? Where do we find the inner strength to do what we know is right in the face of social and financial pressures to do otherwise? There is a parlor game in which people are asked: If you could meet one person from history or literature and ask that person one question, whom would you choose to meet and what question would you ask? Some of the responses I have heard are sincere and thoughtful: "I would ask Jesus if a good person who didn't believe in God could get into heaven." Others are trivial: "I would ask Babe Ruth if he really predicted that home run he hit against the Cubs in the World Series."

The person I would choose to meet would be the prophet Jeremiah, one of my heroes. He lived twenty-six hundred years ago, during the last years of the First Jewish Commonwealth. He saw Solomon's Temple in Jerusalem destroyed by the Babylonians and many of his countrymen exiled to Babylonia. In the years before the fall of Jerusalem, he tried to warn his neighbors that if they did not change their ways, if they did not stop oppressing the poor and worshipping pagan idols instead of God, God would withdraw His protection from the city and the Temple to which His name had been attached. For that, Jeremiah was hated and reviled as a traitor, imprisoned as a security risk. People believed that because he predicted a Babylonian victory he himself favored the Babylonians. He was one of the first great exemplars of the idea that a prophet is not a man who tells the future, he is a man who tells the truth.

Looking back at the history of those times, I see Jeremiah as the person who saved Judaism and made Christianity possible. Had he not sounded that message that the destruction of the Temple was God's chastisement rather than the result of Babylonian military superiority, and had he not offered the possibility of reconciliation with God by changing one's heart and one's behavior, the exiled Judeans might well have concluded that the gods of Babylonia were stronger and offered better protection than the God of Israel. They would have assimilated and become Babylonians, as the defeated and exiled Ammonites and Moabites did, never to be heard of again. There would have been no Jewish people for Jesus to be born into six centuries later.

My question to Jeremiah would be, What did you mean when you said "The word of the Lord came to me . . ."? How does God speak to people? How can you be sure that it is God's voice and not your own wishful thinking? Of the many voices that echo in our minds, how do we recognize which is the authentic voice of God? I would want to know if the feeling of being addressed by God was something that only happened to some two dozen men in ancient times or if it resembles the experience many of us have had when we suddenly felt compelled to do something brave and generous that until that moment we had no intention of doing.

Is it like the feeling I get when I am writing and can't find the words to make a difficult point clear to my readers, and suddenly the perfect phrase, the perfect illustration pops into my head and I find myself wondering how it got there and where it was before I thought of it? Is it like our experience when we are facing a moral dilemma, not sure which is the right choice, and suddenly the fog lifts and we can see the obvious answer staring us in the face? Or is it a totally different experience, unlike anything you and I have ever known?

Jeremiah is the most personally revealing of the prophets. He tells us more about himself than any other biblical author. Listen to how he describes the experience of being a prophet, a spokesman for God: "Lord, You seduced me and I was seduced. You overpowered me and I was overcome. . . . If I say 'I will not speak any more in His name,' there is a fire burning in my heart, within my bones. I exhaust myself trying to hold it in but I cannot." (Jeremiah 20:7–9.) Commenting on that passage, my teacher Abraham Joshua Heschel wrote, "To be a prophet is more than an invitation. It is a sense of yielding to overwhelming force against one's will." Whatever the authentic voice of God is, it is more than wishful thinking. It is more than merely deciding what we want to do and attaching God's name to it.

The twenty-eighth chapter of the book of Jeremiah describes a particularly revealing incident. Jeremiah has made himself the most hated man in Jerusalem by predicting a Babylonian victory. God will not save the people as He has done in the past, because they do not deserve to be saved. Jeremiah has taken to wearing a yoke on his shoulders, like some beast of burden, to symbolize the coming disaster, when the Judeans will have to live under the yoke of Nebuchadnezzar, King of Babylonia. One day, he is confronted by a rival prophet, a man named Hananiah, who takes the yoke off Jeremiah's shoulders and breaks it, proclaiming in the name of the Lord that Babylonia will be defeated and Judea will be saved. To that, Jeremiah, who loves his people though he has been condemning them, answers, "Amen, may the Lord do so." He personally wishes his neighbors no harm and would rather see them victorious, but God's words of chastisement are "a fire burning in [his] heart." He has no choice but to speak them.

After his confrontation with Hananiah, Jeremiah goes home and asks himself, "How can I be sure that I am a true prophet and he is a false one? Why can't I speak words in God's name that will cause people to applaud me and say Amen after me, rather than revile me?" He finds an answer, never explicitly spelled out but implicit in his comments on true and false prophecy: If the words you speak are hard for you to utter and hard for others to hear, if you get no pleasure from speaking them but you feel you must, then you can believe that they come from God. On the other hand, if your words make you popular and win you easy applause, or if people don't like hearing them but you get a certain pleasure from speaking them ("I'm only telling you this for your own good"), then you may have reason to suspect that those are your own thoughts disguising themselves as the Word of God. When I hear politicians and preachers condemning the sinful ways of the society around them, I often agree with their criticisms but I don't hear the pain in their voices. It ought to hurt them more to condemn their neighbors, as it hurt Jeremiah, but they seem too comfortable doing it, and that makes me wonder if they are really bringing us God's words and God's thoughts, or if the words and thoughts are their own.

Some years ago, one of Great Britain's leading Jewish intellectuals was being considered for the position of Chief Rabbi of the British Commonwealth when rumors arose that he was not quite solid enough in his religious faith. An extremely conservative member of the selection committee called him in, opened the Bible to chapter 15 of 1 Samuel, and read Samuel's words to King Saul: "Thus said the Lord of Hosts. . . . Attack Amalek, kill men and women, infants and children, oxen and sheep, sparing no one." The committee member then said to the candidate, "That's in the Bible. Do you believe that God said it to Samuel?" The candidate answered, "I believe that Samuel heard it, but I don't believe that God said it." The authentic voice of God would demand that we be more compassionate and less cruel, that we show more reverence for innocent lives. God always asks more of us, not less. The candidate did not get the position. His questioner chose to believe that God had said what he himself would have said in those circumstances, rather than listen to the challenging voice of compassion.

The voice that commanded Aaron Feuerstein to rebuild Malden Mills, the voice that commands us to volunteer our time at a homeless shelter, the voice that urges us to put the needs and feelings of our family ahead of our own, is the voice of God, because those are things we are unlikely to have thought of on our own. But how did that voice get inside *our* heads? How did God's word take over Jeremiah's mind and heart? Part of the quest for *integrity* includes *integrating* God's will into our conscience, making it the unifying principle of our no-longer-divided soul. Heschel writes of Jeremiah, "The indignation that flowed from him, the anger he displayed, had become so intimate a part of his soul that those exposed to it could easily mistake it as his own anger rather than sympathy with God's anger." But at that point, it *was* his own anger. Jeremiah had made it his own. He had learned to see the world from God's point of view.

The false prophets who invoke God's name to endorse what they are inclined to do anyway, the religious and moral ventriloquists who pretend that God is saying the words that originate with them, are talking to themselves. We can speculate as to whether it was God or wishful thinking when Jacob, the night he ran away from home, dreamed of God reassuring him that things would work out well for him. But we can believe that God was there when Jacob, the night before he was to meet Esau, was attacked by his conscience, struggled all night, and was left limping in the morning. The rule would be: When facing a dilemma, choose the more morally demanding alternative.

The Reverend W. John White, an evangelical pastor, recognized God's voice as he was visiting a colleague in the hospital. White's friend and neighbor Reverend Juan Rivera was seriously ill with kidney failure and had been unable to find a suitable donor for a transplant. White describes what happened in the hospital room: "Juan was unconscious, but I heard a voice literally speaking to me and telling me 'I want you to do whatever it takes to save Juan.' When it became clear that Juan would not live if he did not have the operation, I knew, even without speaking to my wife, what I had to do. I said yes." He donated one of his kidneys.

Sometimes it is more of a struggle to recognize what God would have us do. Remember, Jacob did not simply receive a message from the angel. He wrestled with him. Rabbi Roland Gittelsohn was another of my heroes and a role model for hundreds of young rabbis. His was a voice urging honesty in theology and decency in human relationships. During the Second World War, he was a Marine chaplain who took part in the invasion of Iwo Jima and spoke memorably at the dedication of the Marine cemetery there after the battle, expressing the hope that, in the America to which the soldiers would be returning, blacks and whites, Jews and Christians would be as close and as mutually dependent in peacetime as they had been in combat. Gittelsohn wrote of his decision to become a military chaplain in a passage that could have come from the book of Jeremiah:

It was the most excruciating moral dilemma of my life, one which obsessed me by day and kept me awake a good part of each night. Since my high school days I had been an absolute pacifist. I rationalized moreover that at such a time of severe social crisis, my civilian congregants needed me more than ever. On the other hand, we were involved in a war which might well determine the survival of Judaism and the Jewish people. In addition, young men from my congregation were being drafted; they did not enjoy my luxury of voluntary choice. What did I owe them? I prayed then, more frequently and probably more fervently than ever before. Gradually, in those moments of prayer I moved (or was moved?) toward a solution. I began to feel a Presence in my life, which I had recognized before as a cosmic quality but never felt so immediately within my own mind and heart. Slowly an understanding developed that my decision was related to the very purpose for which the human adventure on this planet had been initiated. I was being tested as God's partner.

For the spiritually authentic person, God is real, not a label we brazenly attach to our own wishes and opinions. God is out there, but through a miracle of divine communication, God's words move from out there to in here, and after a struggle, God's will becomes our will. We will have integrated God's perspective into our own thinking, and achieved integrity. It is the struggle, the feeling that God's demands are at least a little bit unwelcome, that gives us reason to believe that the voice inside our head is God's voice, or God's voice speaking as our voice, and not merely our own. And when the struggle is over, it is the sense that God's voice has become our voice, God's will has been integrated into our will, which lets us know we have won the prize of integrity.

Often this prize reveals itself in seemingly small ways. A friend of mine remembers something that happened more than thirty years ago, when his wife was expecting their first child. She woke up at three o'clock in the middle of a rainy night craving a chocolate bar with almonds. My friend got dressed and went out looking for an all-night convenience store, a drugstore, any place where he could buy a chocolate bar at that hour. After much futile driving around, he found a vending machine in a hotel lobby that offered what he was looking for. What he remembers most about that evening is that he did not resent his wife's request in the least. On the contrary, because he loved her and was excited by her pregnancy, he was happy for the opportunity to please her. Had his soul been divided, he would have felt resentment and obligation along with the pleasure. But he had integrated himself into the marriage to the point where he could banish any sense of resentment and feel only delight. The man or woman who has met the angel and achieved a sense of integrity knows what it feels like to love God and to love the right course of action to that degree.

Did you notice something that Bruce Butterfield, the *Boston Globe* writer I quoted earlier, said about Aaron Feuerstein? He wrote of Feuerstein battling "insurance companies, government officials, competitors out to steal his customers, his own managers *and even himself....*" (Italics added.) Feuerstein is not a saint. He is a *mensh,* a good person. A saint would never be tempted to take the easy way, the more profitable way, enriching himself at the expense of others. A *mensh* would be sorely tempted but would resist the temptation. He would struggle with temptation but would prevail. He would let the angel win. Like Jeremiah, he would recognize the dominating voice inside his head as his own true voice, speaking God's words, and he would have no choice but to obey.

The writer Isaac Bashevis Singer won the Nobel Prize for Literature in 1978 for his novels and short stories about Jewish life in Eastern Europe and among immigrants to the United States. My favorite among his writings, and his most frequently anthologized story, is "Gimpel the Fool." Gimpel is a hardworking baker in a small East European Jewish village. He is an orphan, somewhat simple-minded, and utterly innocent about the capacity of people to be cruel to each other. The townspeople are constantly playing tricks on him, telling him fantastic stories and pretending to be offended when he is skeptical: Are you calling me a liar? They rush into his bakery, for example, and tell him that the Messiah has come and revived the dead and his deceased parents are waiting for him at his home, and laugh at him when he hurries home to look for them.

Gimpel goes to see the town rabbi, who tells him, "Better to be a fool all your days than to be an evil person for one hour. You are not a fool. They are the fools. Anyone who causes his neighbor to feel shame forfeits his place in the World to Come." Gimpel is comforted by these words, but even there, as he leaves the rabbi's house, the rabbi's daughter plays a trick on him and laughs at his gullibility.

The town elders persuade Gimpel to marry a notoriously mean-spirited and promiscuous woman, who would otherwise have no prospects of marriage. Four months later, she gives birth to a son and convinces Gimpel that he has no reason to doubt he is the father. Over the course of their marriage, she betrays him repeatedly. When caught, she takes advantage of his gullible nature to convince him that she has done nothing wrong. At one point, Gimpel muses, "Another man in my place would have left, but I'm the type that bears it and says nothing. God gives us burdens and God gives us shoulders."

Years later, his wife grows ill and is dying. On her deathbed, she confesses everything, saying, "All I ever did in my life was to betray Gimpel, and now my life is over."

Forced to confront the reality of how he has been treated, Gimpel is stunned. He begins to wonder if he was wrong to follow the rabbi's guidance, to be honest and trusting despite the dishonesty of others. A few nights after his wife's death, Gimpel has a dream in which the Evil Impulse whispers to him, "The whole world has deceived you. Now it is time for you to deceive the world. There is no God, there is no World to Come. They have sold you a bill of goods." Realizing that his is the only bakery in town and all the people who mistreated him eat his bread, Gimpel plans revenge. He adds to his dough a mixture of dirt and human waste, to poison and sicken those who have made fun of him. He goes to sleep, planning to wake early and bake those special loaves.

That night, his wife comes to him in a dream, dressed in rags, her face blackened by fire. She tells him, "Because I was false, does that make everything else false? I never deceived anyone but myself and now I am paying for it." Gimpel wakes up, embarrassed by what he was planning to do. Realizing he does not want to be that kind of person, he buries the contaminated dough, locks his bakery, and leaves town. He spends the rest of his days wandering. As he grows old and senses that death is near, he thinks to himself, "Whatever may be on the other side, it will be real, without ridicule, without deception. There, thank God, even Gimpel cannot be fooled."

Gimpel is a man who has very little in life—no wealth, no intellectual gifts, no friends, not even a normal family life.

But he has a certain naïve integrity, and that alone makes him richer than his neighbors. He will not lie, though they lie. He will not hurt another person, though others do not hesitate to hurt him. In the end, we are left with the conclusion that the rabbi was right. The other people were the fools, forfeiting their place in heaven, whatever that may be, because they abused another human being.

Singer's story was originally written in Yiddish. The title of the story in its English version, "Gimpel the Fool," puts it in the tradition of the folktales of the "holy fool," the person of simple faith whose uncomplicated joy at being in the presence of God is more authentically religious than the prayers and sermons of learned theologians. It has its roots in societies that saw the mentally ill not as sick but as having access to a truth different from, but just as valid as, the truth possessed by rational thinkers. It calls to mind plays, most notably Shakespeare's *King Lear,* in which the fool sees the truth more clearly than anyone else.

In the same tradition are the Hasidic tale of the illiterate shepherd who does not know the prayers but recites the alphabet and asks God to arrange the letters into eloquent words, and the story "Our Lady's Juggler," the account of the simple believer who felt sad because he had no gift to bring the Virgin on her holiday, so he shared with her the only gift he had: He juggled before her to bring her cheer. For the reader who grows impatient with Gimpel for his long-suffering passivity, Singer would suggest that there is something holy about Gimpel's foolishness. There is a place in heaven for fools like Gimpel, whereas heaven's gates will be closed to the clever, cruel, and calculating people who embittered his life.

But the title of the story in its original Yiddish version is even more revealing: "Gimpel Tam." *Tam* is a word of Hebrew origin meaning "plain, simple, uncomplicated." Some Jewish readers may recognize it as describing one of the Four Sons of the Passover Haggadah: "The simple child's question is: What is all this?" The word *tam* is related to the important biblical Hebrew word *tamim,* which means "whole, intact," with connotations of integrity. Gimpel is a simple man not only because he is naïve and foolish. He is simple rather than complex. He is not a man of many parts, sometimes honest, sometimes devious, sometimes trusting, sometimes skeptical. His simplicity is that he is the same person all the time. He has very little to his name except his integrity, and though few of us would be inclined to take Gimpel as a role model for our own lives, that integrity, Singer would have us believe as the story ends, is more than any other character has.

The word *tam* appears nine times in the Hebrew Bible. We find it once in the Psalms, once in the book of Proverbs, and six times in the book of Job, where it is used to describe Job as a good, upright, blameless man. In each of those eight passages, it is translated "blameless," a description that would have fit the innocence and naïve integrity of Singer's character Gimpel. It occurs once more in the Torah, the first five books of the Hebrew canon, which Jews consider the holiest part of Scripture. Would you like to guess which biblical hero is characterized as *tam*? Genesis 25:27 reads, "Esau was a skillful hunter, a man of the field, while Jacob was a simple man, dwelling in tents."

Jacob a simple man? The young Jacob plain and uncomplicated, notable for his integrity? Jacob is probably the most complicated, the most devious (and for that reason the most interesting) of all biblical heroes. Perhaps the Bible, in its use of that word to characterize Jacob, is describing the innocence of Jacob as a child, or perhaps it is not so much describing him as he is at the moment as it is foreshadowing who he will become.

The great adventure of Jacob's life will be the effort to climb the ladder that appears to him in his first dream, a ladder reaching from earth to heaven, bridging the gap between the potential for integrity that the Bible sees in the young Jacob and the fulfillment of that potential. Years later, Jacob will shed his earlier self like a snake shedding its skin, so that he can grow. He will struggle with the better angel of his nature, at first resisting the summons to become the person he is capable of becoming, but ultimately giving in, even as Jeremiah resisted the summons to be a prophet but ultimately yielded, accepting the pain and the criticism it entailed and going on to change the world.

Jacob, like so many of us, begins as *tam,* naïve, trusting.

The circumstances of his life will make him in turn deceitful, cynical, and manipulative. But one night, he will meet his angel. He will emerge from the struggle injured and exhausted, limping on to the next chapter of his life. And now the Bible will describe him as *shalem,* whole, united within himself, his internal conflicts ended. He has become a person of integrity.

CHAPTER 6

Family and Friends:
We Are Who We Love

The Bible divides the narrative of Jacob's life into three acts, much as we would divide the story of our own lives. Act One is about Jacob as a youngster, defined primarily by whose child he is. Act Two tells us about Jacob as a young man, defined primarily by whose husband he is. Act Three shows us Jacob as an adult, defined by whose father he is.

If Jacob's life (or our lives) were presented on the stage, the several acts would be separated by the lowering of a curtain and possibly by an intermission, to mark the transition from one time period to another. But because the biblical narrative proceeds in an uninterrupted flow (the division into chapters came much later), it uses a pair of literary devices instead of a curtain. Jacob's childhood is separated from the years of transformation by the dream of the ladder, and the years of withdrawal are marked off from the years of emergence as a person of integrity by the encounter with the angel.

Jacob's dream serves to answer two questions that were tormenting him at the time, two questions that every adolescent is constantly asking himself or herself: Where am I going with my life? What kind of person will I grow up to be? In the dream, God assures Jacob that he will find favor in God's sight, he will outgrow his embarrassing habits and be a good person. And God promises Jacob that he will go on to be successful, that he will matter to the world.

It is, of course, exactly the message Jacob needs to hear at that moment. I have known many an adolescent, myself among them, who was redeemed from self-doubt by hearing that same message from a parent, a teacher, a friend: You are a good person despite some of the things you've done, and you can grow up to be somebody who matters.

Spurred by the reassuring promise of that dream, the first thing that Jacob does is fall in love and marry. He arrives at the well in his uncle Laban's village, sees an attractive young woman watering her flock, learns that she is his cousin Rachel, and impulsively kisses her. Shortly afterward, he asks for her hand in marriage.

(Jacob's parents' marriage had been arranged at that same well, but in very different circumstances. Isaac never met his wife before the wedding. Abraham's servant saw Rebecca at the well and spoke to her family on Isaac's behalf.)

As I mentioned earlier, Jacob is the first, virtually the only, biblical figure to fall romantically in love with someone and set out to marry her. We can see it as the natural ripening of a young man's desire, a young man with no parents nearby to arrange a match for him. We can also see it as fulfilling the expectation of a culture that encouraged young people to marry as soon as they came of age, a culture in which dating and other forms of premarital sexual exploration were unknown. But it would be equally correct to see Jacob's behavior as a response to his dream. If he is to climb the ladder from where he is to where God wants him to be, one of the things he must do is outgrow his habit of relying on himself alone and learn to let other people into his life. The theologian William J. Everett defines sin as "rejecting relationships, both private and public, in which we affirm our own dignity and respect the dignity of the other." A sinner, he says, is "a soul enclosed in the prison of the self." Or as Dostoyevsky put it, "Hell is the suffering of being unable to love." Jacob's love for Rachel, his willingness to sacrifice, to work unpaid for seven years in the service of that love (this is the young man who would not give his brother a bowl of stew without getting something in return), and his discovery that Rachel reciprocates his love are the beginning of the process of Jacob's growing up and becoming a more likable and honorable person. It takes the presence of another person in Jacob's life, someone whose love is reliable and for whose sake he will change, to bring that transformation about.

In Jacob's opening his life to another person, we find the answer to the question of the rock-and-roll singer, "Why do fools fall in love?" Why do we make ourselves vulnerable to pain and loss by letting ourselves care so much for someone? To love another person—husband, wife, or child—is to become a "hostage to fortune." So many things can happen when we take off the armor that protects us and make ourselves vulnerable to being hurt.

Why do we so eagerly expose ourselves to the process of searching and rejection, a process that leaves so many adolescents and young adults feeling that their lives are hopeless because they have not managed to find someone who will love them? If it were only a matter of perpetuating the species, of gratifying our sexual instinct, we could spare ourselves the frustration and anguish of courtship, jealousy, betrayal, and all that is part of the human mating process. In Aldous Huxley's novel *Brave New World,* his frightening vision of a world where all are happy because they have no dreams and no longings, the government has separated sex from reproduction. Children are conceived in laboratories, and sex is purely a form of recreation, never problematic, never emotionally important. At one point, people discover a copy of Shakespeare's *Othello* and can't understand it. What is the matter with that man, getting upset because his wife may have slept with somebody else? Why make yourself unhappy over it?

Why do we set ourselves up for anguish and rejection?

Why are parents and children so emotionally enmeshed with each other, with the power to generate more pride and inflict more guilt and pain on each other than people in any other relationship? Why can't we do as other animals do and send our offspring out into the world as soon as they are old enough to walk, never to see them again? Why is love, the search for love and the pain of loving, the subject of so many songs, so many soap operas, most movies, and all-too-many attempted suicides? We do what we do because for us love is more than reproduction. Love is more than sexual gratification. Love, expressed primarily but not exclusively in marriage and parenthood, is the most accessible way we have of being supremely important in another person's life. It not only gratifies our sex drive and reproductive impulse. It meets our need to matter, or, as one person put it, "to be somebody's somebody."

Writers on health and happiness have suggested that there is a basic human need for intimacy, that our souls are emotionally starved when we deal with strangers all day long. We need people in our lives who know us thoroughly and care about us. Dr. Dean Ornish writes, "Our survival depends on the healing power of love, intimacy and relationships." We need to feel loved. We need people to tell us that we are special and irreplaceable, people who will tend to our needs and banish our fears and insecurities the way our mothers did when we were infants. But we also need to give love, to make a difference in someone's life.

Adolescents desperately crave relationships to counteract the first of Jacob's fears, the fear that they are flawed people and therefore no one will love them. When they, like Jacob, are embarrassed by hurtful things they have done, when they are having problems with parents and siblings, they need the reassurance that somebody somewhere finds them likable. But they ultimately evolve to a more mature understanding of love, one that deals with the second part of Jacob's dream, the need to matter, to make a difference in another person's life. They come to understand that love involves nourishing someone else's soul and not only finding someone willing to nourish yours. Ornish writes, "I used to feel I was loved because I was special. Now I feel special because I am loved and because I *can* love."

In the 1970s, the congregation I was serving was afflicted with a plague of marital breakdowns. Once or twice a month, I would hear of a husband and wife separating and heading for divorce. It got to the point where nearly half of the thirteen-year-olds celebrating a bar mitzvah had to deal with having parents come to the ceremony from different homes. I began to understand something of the dynamics of divorce and marital breakdown. I learned that sometimes marriages fail because one or both partners are not receiving the love they need, but sometimes a marriage fails when one partner is frustrated in his or her need to *give* love, to make a difference in another person's life.

I remember a woman in my community who would periodically come to me to complain about her marriage, telling me that she had to do everything around the house, that her husband was uninvolved with the children, that he was emotionally distant. I tried to be sympathetic, always reminding myself that I was hearing only one side of the story, and from time to time I would ask her why she stayed in such an unsatisfying marriage. Her answer was that she didn't have the heart to leave her husband. He would be helpless without her. His life would be empty.

Then, one day, she came to me in tears. He had left her. His parting words were that he wanted to be more of a husband and more of a father, and she wouldn't let him. Those roles didn't come easily to him, perhaps because he didn't know how to fulfill them, his own father not having set an example for him. But he felt that, instead of letting him try to learn, his wife chose, for whatever psychological reasons, to claim those areas as her own and leave no space for him.

We marry for intimacy, to find someone who will care for us. We marry for sexual access, in response to strong natural urges. But we also marry to join ourselves to someone whose life will be different for having shared life with us. We have children to achieve biological immortality or to meet family and societal expectations. But we also have children to claim the opportunity to shape another person's life. We work to earn money to pay our bills. But many of us also work to make a difference to the world in some small way. We emerge from the chrysalis of adolescent self-involvement feeling the need to be important to the world, to be noticed (whereas the typical adolescent dreads being noticed), and to be significant. Many, perhaps all, of us have echoed the sentiments of the English writer Joseph Addison: "If I can in any way contribute to the improvement of the country in which I live, I shall leave this life when I am summoned out of it with the satisfaction of knowing that I have not lived in vain."

We cannot live without the knowledge that someone cares about us, and marriage provides the most accessible, though not the only, way of having that need met. That may be why recent efforts to create alternatives to marriage—communes with interchangeable partners, couples living together without ceremony and with both partners having the freedom to leave whenever they feel their needs are not being met— have never managed to be as nourishing to the soul as the thousands-of-years-old institution of marriage. They carry a message of "you can be replaced" instead of "you matter to me more than anyone else in the world." That may also be why infidelity has more power to destroy a marriage than any other failing, more than criminal activity, mental illness, or obnoxious personal behavior. It says, "Someone else is more important to me in the most intimate moments of my life than you are." (Interestingly, men caught in extramarital affairs typically try to justify them by denying any emotional involvement: "She doesn't matter to me; it was just a transient physical attraction." A woman typically justifies extra-marital behavior by insisting that she was in love, that her partner in the affair filled some emotional void in her life.)

Several of the prophets of the Hebrew Bible saw the relationship between God and the people of Israel as a kind of marriage. Whereas the prophet Amos sees the Covenant between God and His people as resembling a business agreement, so that violation of the Covenant is a default deserving punishment, his more passionate contemporary Hosea sees it as a marriage bond. Violation of the Covenant is more than default; it is betrayal. Whereas Amos pictures God demanding obedience and saying to Israel, How can I be your God if you don't do what I tell you to?, Hosea imagines a God who wants to love a people and be loved by them. For Hosea, God's plea is, How can I have a true relationship with you if your relationship with God is not the most important thing in your life?

The capacity for friendship seems to be a uniquely human gift. It takes more than one person to validate our sense of mattering to the world. It may be a mistake to rely on one person to meet all of our emotional needs, putting more of a burden on that one, most intimate relationship than it can bear. Our mates may be good at meeting many of our needs, but not all of them. Our relationships with our children may suffer if we ask them to meet our emotional needs at the expense of their growing up to be who they need to be, and our sense of significance is enhanced when we know that we are important to more people than our immediate family. That is why we need friends in our lives.

Animals lower on the environmental scale seem incapable of relationships. Fish and reptiles do not seem able to tell the difference between the young they have just hatched and other newborns, and as anyone with a home fish tank knows, many species of fish eat their young. Only in cartoons do fish and snakes make friends with other fish and snakes. More evolved animals seem capable of more developed emotional lives. Some mate for life and grieve at the death of a member of their group. Young animals will play and romp together, much like young children, and certainly dogs develop a special relationship with their owners. But there doesn't seem to be anything like the emotional bond of sharing thoughts and hopes that characterize the friendship of two people.

What is friendship? *Boston Globe* columnist Ellen Goodman and her best friend of twenty-six years, novelist Patricia O'Brien, wrote a book about what their friendship has meant to them, *I Know Just What You Mean.* They write, "Friendship has no biological purpose, no economic status, no evolutionary meaning." But "a new friend can reintroduce a woman to herself, allowing her to look at herself with a new pair of eyes and a different mindset. . . . Flaws can be recast as strengths, self-doubts lifted by acceptance. . . . Friends are more likely than family to encourage change."

The instinct for friendship seems to be a part of us from an early age. Very young children delight in having a playmate, even before they are old enough to interact with other children. It meets some need of theirs just to have a familiar figure nearby as they play in parallel. Young children, especially girls, will have "best friends" from whom they will be inseparable. (Psychologist-author Carol Gilligan has pointed out that young girls tend to latch on to best friends, as if they were rehearsing for marriage, whereas boys play competitive games with their friends, as if they were rehearsing for the business world.)

A man in my community turned down "the economic opportunity of a lifetime" because it would have meant taking his two teenage daughters out of high school and away from their friends, and moving to a small Southern community where they would be one of the few Jewish families in town. His daughters burst into tears when they heard of the job offer and said they would move in with friends rather than go with him. He contemplated living in the new community alone until the girls finished high school but decided that was unrealistic and said no to the offer. I asked him, "Did you worry that you were giving your teenagers too much power in the family, granting them a virtual veto over your professional life?" He said, "No. Had we all been five years younger, I probably would have taken the job and brought them along kicking and screaming, and I suspect it would have been something I regretted. I might have succeeded in the job at great cost to the people who mean more to me than anything else in my life. I'm glad my family forced me to realize what my priorities were."

Adolescence can be a lonely and frightening country if you don't have your circle of friends to make life bearable. I know one woman, happily married and successful in her field, who still cries when she remembers what it was like in high school to go to the cafeteria at lunchtime and search for a table where other girls would welcome her.

Friendships are a key to survival in an unfriendly world. They are a way for us to be recognized as unique people, to be reassured that we are appreciated for who we are. One step less intense than marriage or parenthood, genuine friendships are a mirror reflecting back to us a flattering image of ourselves. The fact that they are voluntary, easier to enter or leave than family, marriage, or professional relationships, reassures us that people remain our friends because they genuinely like us, even when we have hurt or disappointed them. It has been said, "When a friend makes a mistake, the mistake remains a mistake but the friend is still a friend." And friendships are a way of being important in another person's life, knowing that someone we like and care about is happier, more secure, and more likely to make right choices in his or her life because of us. Patricia O'Brien says of her friend, "With Ellen, I could talk about family and politics and change and loss and get back more than supportive echoes. *More than that, she needed me, which is no small thing.*" (Italics added.)

We never outgrow our need for friendship. Friends are an alternative source of the emotional nourishment we get from our families, in case what we get from our families isn't enough, in case our husbands and wives can only meet some of our emotional needs all of the time and all of our emotional needs some of the time. But there will be things we like about ourselves that friends can reinforce better than our family members can. Human beings are social creatures. We flourish in the company of other human beings. That is why we go to church or synagogue instead of speaking to God in the comfort of our homes, and why we go to the stadium instead of watching a game on television.

I remember only one sentence from an anthropology course I took in college. A man who had spent a lifetime studying chimpanzees in the wild concluded in his book that "one chimpanzee cannot be a chimpanzee." A chimp needs other chimps in order to become what it was meant to be. I don't know if that is really true for chimpanzees (I'll take the author's word for it), but I know it is true for people. We need other people, and we need to be needed by other people, in order to be who we might be, who we yearn to be.

We are who we love. When Jacob could not love, because the circumstances of his growing up had made it hard for him to trust anyone, he could not be Jacob. He could not become Israel, God's champion. Only by letting people into his life could he fulfill his potential.

Recently, three psychiatrists from San Francisco—

Thomas Lewis, Fari Amini, and Richard Lannon—wrote a book entitled *A General Theory of Love,* in which they explore and explain the human need and ability to connect with other people, either romantically or in the bond of friendship. They locate the capacity for love in the limbic brain, the emotional center of our brain, rather than in its rational center. That physical fact explains why we can't talk ourselves or anyone else into loving somebody any more than we can convince ourselves or other people that a certain person is wrong for us or them if the attraction is there. We find ourselves drawn to people for reasons we can't explain. But we need friendship and affection as much as we need food and air, and we identify certain people as able to meet that need. We will be baffled by the friends our children bring home, whether in first grade or their junior year in college, and our children won't be able to explain to us what they see in those friends, but the connections will make emotional sense to them.

One of the saddest commentaries on American life is that we have made it so hard for men to have male friends. We have done such a good job of teaching men that all other men are potential rivals or potential customers, and that they should never expose their vulnerability to another man (which, I suspect, is why men have trouble asking for directions, and why they would rather try to fix something themselves than ask for help). Men have buddies, guys they go fishing with or watch football with. But it is rare for a man to open himself emotionally to another man. Go into a restaurant at lunch hour. If you see two women talking over lunch, chances are they are friends taking time to catch up with each other's lives. If you see two men talking, chances are they are discussing a prospective business deal. I would speculate that a lot of extramarital affairs are the result not of men looking for sex but of men looking for friendship, for a kind of intimacy they don't find with other men. When I have been in settings where men were assured they would be safe if they opened up emotionally—twelve-step groups, the Men's Forum of the Young Presidents Organization—men have seemed so grateful for the opportunity to speak about their fears and their feelings.

Recently, I called a friend to get the address of a mutual acquaintance. By all rights, it should have been a one-minute conversation. But something in his voice prompted me to say, "You sound a little tense. Is everything all right?" For the next ten minutes, he proceeded to tell me about problems with his work and how those problems had revealed fault lines in his marriage to a point where the marriage was in serious trouble. It was frustrating for me not to be able to do anything more helpful than listen, but I would like to think that listening helped, and that being able to penetrate the typical male façade of "I'm okay, just a little distracted" helped as well.

Just as the best present is often not the one you were hinting about but the one you didn't know you wanted until someone gave it to you, the best gift of a friendship will often be the friend's ability to know what you need even before you do. And just as with material gifts, the satisfaction of pleasing someone you care about is as gratifying as the pleasure of discovering how much someone cares about you. Ralph Waldo Emerson put it this way: "The glory of friendship is not so much in the outstretched hand or even in the kindly smile. It is in the spiritual inspiration that comes when you discover that someone else believes in you and is willing to trust you with his friendship."

Friends have been defined as people who know you at your worst and like you anyway, people in whose company you can be yourself. But perhaps more than anything else, friends are people who care about you for who you are, not for what you can do for them. They worry about you when you're sick or depressed, and they rejoice with you when you have something to celebrate. Perhaps the truest friend is the person who can be genuinely happy for you when something good comes your way that may never happen to him or her, whether marriage, financial success, talented children, or any other blessing. There is a kind of holiness in true friendship, because it does for us what organized religion tries to do, to make sure that we are never alone when we desperately need to not be alone.

At some of the darkest moments of my life, some people I thought of as friends deserted me—some because they cared about me and it hurt them to see me in pain; others because I reminded them of their own vulnerability, and that was more than they could handle. But real friends overcame their discomfort and came to sit with me. If they had no words to make me feel better, they sat in silence (much better than saying "You'll get over it," or "It's not so bad; others have it worse"), and I loved them for it.

I can't tell you how often, as a rabbi, I would meet with family members before a funeral and one of them would say to me, "Rabbi, we're not religious. Do we have to observe the *shiva* memorial week and have all those people crowding our living room at a time like this?" And I would tell them, "Yes, you have to do that, not for God's sake but for yours, because you're going to feel alone and abandoned and you need to know that you're not alone. And you need to do it for your friends' sake as well. They feel your pain and want to take some of it onto themselves, to grieve with you."

That is why we have to make room in our lives for people who may sometimes disappoint or exasperate us. If we hold our friends to a standard of perfection, or if they do that to us, we will end up far lonelier than we want to be.

When Martin Buber, the great Jewish philosopher and theologian, was asked "Where is God?" he was wise enough not to give the cliché answers: God is everywhere; God is found in churches and synagogues. Buber would answer that God is found in relationships. God is not found *in* people; God is found *between* people. When you and I are truly attuned to each other, God comes down and fills the space between us so that we are connected, not separated. Both love and true friendship are more than a way of knowing that we matter to someone else. They are a way of mattering to the world, bringing God into a world that would otherwise be a vale of selfishness and loneliness.

CHAPTER 7

Best Actor in a Supporting Role

Whether I shall turn out to be the hero of my own life or whether that station will be held by anybody else, these pages must show.

—Opening line of *David Copperfield,* by Charles Dickens

Every year, on an evening in late March, tens of millions of Americans stay up late to watch the motion-picture industry present its Academy Awards. The coveted Oscars are given to the best director, the best actor and actress, the best movie, and the best in other categories. Among the prestigious awards given out are those for the best male and the best female actor in a supporting role.

I have always been intrigued by the supporting-role category. I don't know what it is like to direct a movie. I have no idea what goes into composing a musical score or designing the costumes. But I know the feeling—I suspect we all know the feeling—of being a supporting actor in other people's movies, not being in the spotlight but doing things that shape and drive the plot. A friend is undergoing chemotherapy for cancer and we visit her, cook a meal for her, drive her to an appointment. Her life is a drama, a life-or-death struggle. We are in the background, doing what we can to make things turn out well. Our church or synagogue undertakes to work with the poor and neglected. We are not prepared to leave our families and move to Haiti or Appalachia, but we contribute what we can afford so that other people will be able to go. The victim of a tragic automobile accident turns out to have registered as an organ donor, and four people are given a new life because of her. Like Dickens's David Copperfield, we may yearn to be the star of the movie of our lives, but most of us will never attain that billing. Others will be at the center of the action, and we will be there in a supporting role, making important things happen in the process.

It is too bad that the movie *It's a Wonderful Life* has become such a cliché of the Christmas season. Like Dickens's *A Christmas Carol* and the cartoons about snowmen and red-nosed reindeer, it is replayed every December until it becomes the cinematic equivalent of the fruitcake that returns every year because nobody wants to eat it. And that is a shame, because, though it is an insufferably corny movie with impossibly noble heroes and irredeemably wicked villains, at the heart of the movie is a valid and vital message.

You may be familiar with the story. James Stewart plays George Bailey, a small-town banker and homebuilder who always does the right and generous thing and whom everybody loves. Through a combination of other people's mistakes and other people's greed, his bank is about to fail. He is distraught, feels like a failure, and contemplates taking his own life. His insurance policy would be enough to cover the bank's shortfall, so he is worth more to his community dead than alive. (The movie never raises the question of whether the policy would pay off for a self-inflicted death.) A guardian angel is sent to rescue him, and when he complains to the angel that the world would be better off if he had never been born, the angel decides to show him what it would be like if he had never existed. Had it not been for George, the local pharmacist, whom he saved from making a terrible mistake with a prescription, would have gone to prison and ended up a broken-down panhandler instead of a prominent member of the community. George's younger brother, whose life he saved in a sledding accident and who went on to become a war hero, would have died at age eight, and the soldiers whose lives he saved would have died young as well. The woman George married would have grown up to be a dowdy old maid had he not been part of her life. The people for whom he financed homes would have gone on living in shanties, and his hometown would have been a much less pleasant place. And, of course, his children, and their future children, would never have been born. The point the movie is (not very subtly) making is that George, who once dreamed of "doing something big and important" and felt like a failure because he thought he hadn't, had in fact done a lot of important things, changing many people's lives for the better. As his guardian angel tells him, "Each man's life touches many others. If he's not there, it leaves a hole."

The angel is right, of course. Dr. Rachel Naomi Remen tells a true story in her book *My Grandfather's Blessings* that parallels the fictional story of George Bailey in the movie. Dr. Remen deals with the spiritual and emotional needs of people with cancer as well as with their physical problems. She had one patient, coincidentally also named George, who had been diagnosed with colon cancer and had only a few months to live. He sat in her office crying because he felt he had wasted his life and that it was now too late to change it. The man was a scientist and an inventor who had made a lot of money inventing and marketing medical devices, but had put so much of himself into his work that he neglected his family. He was estranged from two wives and several grown children. Facing the prospect of dying alone and unmourned, he lamented, "What a fool I've been. All I cared about was making money, and I'll end up leaving it to a bunch of people who don't even like me."

One of the devices he had invented, his most profitable invention, helped people with a chronic illness to live an almost normal life. By coincidence, Dr. Remen had another patient, a young woman, who suffered from that disease and used that device. It enabled her to work, to marry and raise a family. When Dr. Remen told this woman that she knew the man who had invented the device that changed her life, she was stunned and excited. She asked if she could meet him.

What Dr. Remen thought would be a half-hour of small talk and thanks turned out to be an elegant dinner party at which each of the woman's relatives who had nursed her through her illness and seen her return to a normal life spoke of the difference George's invention had made for all of them. George, who had cried in the doctor's office just a few days earlier, cried for a very different reason that evening.

When we worry that our lives are passing in a parade of trivialities and insignificant events, when, like George Bailey, we yearn to do things that matter and feel like failures because we haven't, I have always found that an effective cure for that feeling of insignificance is simply to find someone who needs our help and reach out to that person. A reader wrote to Ann Landers suggesting a cure for teenage moodiness and anger at the world: Get them involved in some form of community service. "Teens who help others are fifty percent less likely to join gangs, use drugs or become pregnant." Their high-school grades are better, and dropout rates are lower. One suspects that a lot of the self-destructive, anti-social behavior of young people, who can be so beautifully idealistic, arises to fill the vacuum of their feeling that they have nothing important to do. Giving them something to do, making them feel important in somebody's life (and isn't that why so many teenage girls become sexually active at a young age, to feel important to somebody?), makes them feel better about themselves.

Reading Tom Brokaw's book *The Greatest Generation,*

which consists of recollections of men and women who fought in the Second World War, I was struck by the tone that pervaded so many of those memories. The experiences these soldiers and nurses recalled were often horrible. Torn from the security of home and hometown, they were sent off to fight in Europe or the Pacific. They lived in mud and cold. Many of them were wounded; virtually all saw friends die. But the book is strikingly free of complaint and self-pity. Instead, what comes through is a sense of pride in having done something that changed the world for the better. Only a few of the men and women interviewed in the book were generals, admirals, or Medal of Honor winners. Most of them were plain soldiers, sailors, pilots, and nurses, men and women "just doing their job," and in the process saving the world for democracy.

The need to feel useful and important continues into the last part of life. One of the most shameful aspects of our society is the way it makes elderly people feel useless because they (like so many teenagers) are neither attractive nor productive, and those are the qualities our society worships. We are embarrassed, even frightened, by the elderly in part because they remind us that one day we will grow old and lose the qualities that cause others to admire us. But if we could tap into the accumulated wisdom and experience of the elderly, if we could give them not shuffleboard and occupational therapy but the opportunity to be truly useful—for example, as surrogate grandparents for children whose grandparents have died or live thousands of miles away—it would be a blessing to all parties involved.

I have visited communities in Florida populated almost entirely by elderly widows and widowers doing nothing but killing time, watching television programs whose dialogue they can't hear, shopping for cosmetics they don't need, just to have something to do. And I have visited other communities where the elderly go into the public schools to serve lunches and tutor children with reading problems, and where students from a local college interview them for an oral-history documentary about what life was like in America in the early twentieth century.

Psychologist Erik Erikson has written that people approaching the last chapters of their lives have to choose between stagnation and generativity. He defines stagnation as thinking only about ourselves: How do I feel today? What aches? Who calls me, and who ignores me? Generativity is worrying about the next generation and what sort of world we are leaving them. Needless to say, generativity is the healthy choice. It pulls us out of ourselves and gives us a role to play in the world.

To be somebody's somebody: There are so many ways to do that. I am often invited to speak to groups of teachers and educators at their conferences, usually on a topic like "The Classroom as Sacred Space." When I do, I always save the last ten or fifteen minutes to talk to them about the danger of burnout, feeling worn down by the stresses of the job and losing enthusiasm for the teaching profession. I tell them that burnout results not from hard work—people are capable of working very hard—but from a sense of futility, the fear that all the hard work isn't making a difference. And the cure for burnout among teachers, I tell them, is to help them realize how much of a difference they do make in people's lives, even if no one bothers to thank them.

We have all read interviews with a man or woman who has climbed out of the inner-city ghetto and gone on to do great things. The interviewer will ask, "How did you do it? You began in such discouraging circumstances—absentee father, mother on welfare, gangs and drug dealers in the streets. And you went on to become a doctor, a scholar, a professional athlete, a member of Congress, a role model for thousands. How did you manage it?" The answer will always begin with the same four words: "There was this teacher. . . ." Somewhere along the way, a teacher noticed a spark of promise in a girl, a light in her eyes. The teacher spent extra time with her, lent her books, reached into her own purse for snacks or materials, and affected not just one life but countless others.

Every clergyman I know has had the experience I've had. A person will come up and tell me, "You said something in a sermon ten years ago that changed my life." He will quote something that I may not even remember having said, but he remembers it ten years later. And for every time someone goes to the trouble of thanking a clergyman, a teacher, or a doctor, there must be dozens, even hundreds, of people who should speak those words but don't. I once sat on a committee awarding college scholarships to outstanding high-school seniors. One impressive young man told the committee that he had been accepted at Harvard, where he was going to major in anthropology. I asked him: "Why anthropology? That seems like an unusual choice." He replied: "I had this really great anthropology course in high school. It was the most exciting course I ever took. I decided that was where I wanted to go with my life." I asked him: "Did you ever tell that teacher what his course meant to you? I suspect it would mean a lot to him to know." He answered ruefully: "No, I never did. I probably should have."

In the Bible, there is a strange incident involving Jacob's sons. Because Joseph, the son of Jacob's beloved wife, Rachel, is his father's favorite, his brothers are jealous of him. One day, when the brothers are out pasturing the sheep some distance from home, Jacob sends Joseph out to make sure everything is all right. Joseph cannot find them, but he meets a man in the field who asks him, "What are you looking for?" When Joseph tells him that he is looking for his brothers, the man says, "Oh yes, I heard them say 'Let's move on to Dothan [a nearby city].'" Joseph finds them there, and they, in a fit of jealous rage, sell him to a passing caravan as a slave. (One scholar notes that Dothan was a big city, not pastureland, and wonders if the brothers sold Joseph into slavery not only out of jealousy but because he had caught them neglecting the flocks for the pleasures of the city.) Joseph is taken to Egypt, where he becomes Pharaoh's chief minister, guiding Egypt through a famine. His brothers come to Egypt to buy food, and the biblical story proceeds from there.

But where did that man in the field come from? The Bible rarely wastes words. There are minor characters in the biblical narrative, but no superfluous characters. What is the significance of that man whom Joseph meets? Some commentators identify him as an angel sent by God to make sure that Joseph would find his brothers and fulfill his destiny. They may be right, if we understand an angel to be not a winged figure from heaven but a messenger sent into our lives to nudge us in the direction we need to go.

If Joseph had not encountered that man, he would not have known that his brothers had moved from their usual place. He would have had no idea where to find them, and would have turned around and gone home. Joseph might well have been ambivalent about visiting his brothers and might have seized on any excuse to avoid them. He would not have been grabbed by his brothers and sold to a caravan headed for Egypt. Pharaoh would never have had Joseph's advice, which made Egypt the only place in the Near East with abundant grain during the famine. Jacob's family would never have migrated to Egypt. The Israelite people would never have been enslaved. There would have been no Moses, no Exodus, no Ten Commandments. The history of the world would have been radically different.

Did the man in the field even remember meeting a teenage boy who couldn't find his brothers and having a one-sentence conversation with him? And if he did remember, could he possibly imagine that that one-sentence conversation would change history? Could Dr. Remen's patient, studying his company's balance sheet and calculating how many medical devices he had sold, comprehend how many people and their families would have reason to bless his name for the quality of their lives? Could a schoolteacher in Brooklyn or in North Carolina realize how a few words of encouragement to a child whose name she can't even remember would go on to affect the lives of millions? And what of the angels who came into our lives—the friend who brought us to a party where we met the person we would marry; the neighbor who recommended a book that helped us understand ourselves and our family better; the man who left a newspaper on a park bench, in which we found an article or help-wanted notice that changed our lives? Every life touches many other lives, and rare is the person who knows how much of a difference he or she has made.

Can one ordinary person really change things? Can we, in our anonymity, affect history? Rarely can we, by what we do alone, move mountains and make a difference. But by being good people and doing good things, we can, as members of a community dedicated to goodness, change the world. We can matter.

I learned that lesson from the 1985 movie *Witness,* which

tells the story of a twelve-year-old boy from an Amish community in rural Pennsylvania who witnesses a murder in the restroom of a railroad terminal. Harrison Ford plays the detective assigned to protect the boy from the killers who know that he can identify them. Ford discovers that the murder was carried out by corrupt policemen, colleagues of his, and he becomes their next target. He goes into hiding among the Amish. The villains find out where he is and come after him.

Peter Weir, the director of *Witness,* is an Australian who was apparently raised on American Western movies. Some early scenes, like the one in which the young boy is fascinated by Ford's skill with a gun, resemble scenes in *Shane,* and much of the climactic showdown echoes the classic Gary Cooper movie *High Noon.* There is a moment when the three intimidating villains appear over the crest of a hill, carrying their guns, as menacing music blares. There is another scene, shortly afterward, in which Ford is trapped in a barn and escapes by hanging over the side of a horse so that he can't be seen, exactly as Cooper did in *High Noon* (and as Odysseus did in Homer's *Odyssey*).

Many moviegoers watching *Witness* and remembering *High Noon* must have thought, as I did, that they knew what was going to happen next. In *High Noon,* Cooper's pacifist Quaker wife, played by Grace Kelly, overcomes her opposition to violence, grabs a gun, and shoots the last of the bad men before he can shoot her husband. The moral is that sometimes you have to violate your most cherished beliefs and compromise your integrity to keep the bad guys from winning. You have to fight fire with fire and use evil methods to defeat evil.

Watching *Witness,* we are aware that the boy knows where Ford's gun is hidden, and we expect him to violate his community's beliefs about guns, get the weapon, and save his protector, just as Grace Kelly did. But Weir surprises us. The boy runs not for the gun but for the town bell, summoning all the farmers from the fields. The hundred unarmed men stare down the villains, conveying the message We will not permit this evil to be perpetrated in our midst. The corrupt police cannot resist the collective moral force of an entire community.

High Noon was made in 1952, when Hollywood was reeling from the impact of blacklisting and congressional investigations of alleged communist influence in the movie industry. The film's message was: You can't count on your neighbors to help you, and you may have to do things you don't believe in to save yourself. *Witness* was filmed in the more optimistic year 1985, and its message was: One man alone can't defeat the forces of evil, but many good people coming together can.

I believe that. I believe that ordinary people joining forces can do things that heroes acting alone can't do. I believe that shame can often be a more effective deterrent to wrongdoing that the threat of legal punishment. As I suggested earlier, we all need to think of ourselves as good people, and the judgment of our neighbors means a lot to us.

In the 1980s, Native Americans living on the Pine Ridge reservation in South Dakota were facing a problem of domestic violence. Men fueled by alcohol or frustration were physically abusing their wives and children. There were too few police, with too little control, to deal with the situation. In desperation, the tribal elders tried an old remedy, shame. Any man who struck his wife or child would be shunned by his neighbors. For a repeat offense, he would be banished to a mountaintop for a three-day fast, and the men in the tribe would make sure he stayed up there and fasted. As in *Witness,* the community said, louder and more effectively than the law could, We are not going to put up with this.

The Talmud tells of one of the sages who was close to death. His students gathered around his bed, urging him to leave them with one last bit of wisdom. He said to them, "May you fear God as much as you fear men." The students were perplexed. One of them said, "Master, has illness confused your mind? Surely you mean to say that we should fear God more than we fear people." "No, my son," the sage replied, "so many people do things of which they know God disapproves but go to great lengths to hide them from their neighbors. If only they feared God as much."

Communal standards and communal pressure, the combined force of good people banding together, will do more to curb wrong behavior than either sermons or threats of jail. What one person alone cannot do, many of us together are often able to achieve.

The Israeli writer S. Y. Agnon was awarded the Nobel Prize for Literature in 1966, honoring him for his novels and short stories, which are written in a dense, richly textured Hebrew. A typical Agnon story seems, at first reading, to be deceptively simple and old-fashioned. Only a closer examination reveals how subtle a tale it really is.

When the son of Agnon's publisher reached the age of thirteen and became a bar mitzvah, Agnon's present to the boy was a short story, thirteen chapters long, called "The Kerchief." When my son Aaron became a bar mitzvah, my sermon that Sabbath was based on the Agnon story.

In "The Kerchief," the narrator remembers how his mother had an especially beautiful kerchief that she would wear only on Sabbaths and holidays, as she lit the festive candles. Because it was used only then, it remained immaculately clean. When the narrator reaches the age of bar mitzvah, his mother gives him the kerchief, much as Jewish parents today might give their thirteen-year-old son a prayer shawl to wear at services. It becomes his most cherished possession. He regards it as a holy object, and tries to keep it immaculate, as his mother had done.

In Hebrew school, the boy learns the legend of the Messiah traveling the world disguised as a beggar dressed in rags, waiting for someone to recognize him and reach out to him, at which point he will reveal himself and redeem the world from sickness and misery. Shortly after that, the boy sees a beggar in rags, his feet sore and bleeding, at the entrance to the town. Impulsively, he gives the beggar his mother's kerchief, and the beggar gratefully uses it to wrap his wounds. The boy goes home, feeling guilty for having permitted his mother's precious kerchief to be soiled, and vaguely disappointed that the beggar did not turn out to be the Messiah and that the world is still not redeemed. But as he walks home, the sun shines warmly on him, signifying heaven's approval of what he has done, and he can see his mother smiling at him.

I met Agnon once, when I was studying in Israel, and asked him a question about the meaning of one of his stories. He answered, "I only write stories; I leave it to the critics to explain them." But even without Agnon spelling out the moral, we can understand what his story is about. The boy, an idealistic adolescent, wants to redeem the world. He wants to be the hero who will usher in the messianic age. To make that happen, he does the bravest, most generous thing he can do. And when he has done it, the world is still not redeemed. Or is it? What happens to the beggar at the end of the story? Does he come to see the world differently because suddenly, in his pain and abandonment, a child appears and gives him a fine cloth to bind his bleeding feet? Does the world suddenly become a warmer and friendlier place for him? And, whatever might happen to him in the future, will he always remember that brief moment of kindness?

As I suggested in my sermon on the Sabbath of my son's bar mitzvah, no matter how much we would like to, we can't bring the Messiah and solve the world's problems. Nor can we bring the Messiah for ourselves and solve our own problems. But maybe we can bring the Messiah for someone else. We can be the supporting actor who gives someone else's life story a happy ending, and we can hope that someone will come along and do the same for us. (As some readers may know, my wife and I lost our son a year after he became bar mitzvah, of a rare, incurable growth disorder. He could not bring the Messiah for himself, but he did for others. More than half of his classmates remembered him in their college applications as "the most unforgettable person I have ever met," and wrote of how they were inspired to handle their own problems by seeing how he coped with his.)

My friend and colleague Rabbi Lawrence Kushner (no relation, but a neighbor and fellow author) has written: "Each lifetime is the pieces of a jigsaw puzzle. For some, there are more pieces. For others, the puzzle is more difficult to assemble. But know this: you do not have within yourself all the pieces to your puzzle. Everyone carries with them at least one and probably many pieces to someone else's puzzle. Sometimes they know it; sometimes they don't know it. And when you present your piece, which is worthless to you, to another, whether you know it or not, whether they know it or not, you are a messenger from the Most High."

There is one other way in which our souls' craving for significance is met. I believe that, whoever we are and however much or little we accomplish in our lives, we matter to God. Our relationship to God is not that of slaves to a master who demands obedience, but of students to a master Teacher who would tell us how to live. When God tells us not to steal or commit adultery, when God forbids us to cheat the blind or shame the poor, it is not because He wants to restrict our choices in life. It is because He wants us to know the enduring satisfaction of living as people were meant to live. When I, as an observant Jew, refrain from eating certain foods and from working on the Sabbath, I don't feel deprived, I feel exalted. Ostensibly trivial things like my choice at lunch or my decision to read for pleasure on the Sabbath rather than write to deadline are transformed into religious affirmations, moments of connecting with God. God has shown me how to invest the most mundane moments of my life with holiness.

Oscar Wilde once wrote, "The nicest feeling in the world is to do a good deed anonymously—and have somebody find out." Strip that statement of its cynicism and I would agree with it. One of the important messages I get from my religious view of life is that, when I do something kind and thoughtful, or when I don't do something mean and hurtful—the temptation I resist, the angry words I don't speak—and nobody applauds me for it, Somebody knows what I've done. The assurance that how I earn and spend my money matters at the highest level, that what sort of language I use with my children and whom I sleep with affect the world in some small but real way, invests my life with significance. I matter.

The book of Job, the Bible's classic discussion of the good man who suffers and asks "Why?," has always spoken to me. But I have never been sure that I understood the ending. For thirty-five chapters of glorious theological poetry, Job, the victim of misfortune he does not deserve, demands that God explain to him what he has done to deserve his suffering. Then, at the end of the book, God appears. But instead of answering Job's question, instead of explaining why bad things happen to good people, God speaks about a lot of other things: Were you there when I created the world? Do you know when the mountain goats give birth to their young? Can you catch the sea monster Leviathan? And Job, for some reason, is satisfied with God's response.

Hundreds of scholars, over thousands of years, have tried to make sense of the book's ending. Is God cowing Job into submission by this awesome display of might, telling him, in effect, "Shut up! This is my world"? Is God saying that the fate of one human being is not all that important in this vast universe? Is God admitting that life is not fair?

I have come to believe that the author of the book is telling us that Job is satisfied not by God's words but by God's appearance. It is the *contact,* not the *content* of God's speech that answers his questions and eases his doubts. God knows Job's name, and that is answer enough for him.

To know that we matter to God makes a lot of our doubts and fears disappear. We don't have to find the cure for cancer to make a difference to the world, and we don't have to write great novels to be noticed by God. We only have to share our lives with other people, and choose generativity over stagnation. As Mother Teresa said, "Few of us can do great things, but all of us can do small things with great love." We are the supporting cast of a great and ongoing drama, and it is our inestimable privilege to be part of it.

CHAPTER 8

Why We Matter to the World

Over the course of my thirty years as a congregational rabbi, I have seen many people come to the end of their lives. I have held their hands and prayed with them on the eve of a desperate, last-chance operation. I have seen them deteriorate from week to week from the effects of a debilitating illness. I have seen courage, love, and humor in the face of death. The dying have taught me one great lesson that I never would have learned without their help: Most people are not afraid of dying; they are afraid of not having lived. As I suggested at the beginning of the book, it is not the prospect of death that frightens most people. People can accept the inescapable fact of mortality. What frightens them more is the dread of insignificance, the notion that we will be born and live and one day die and none of it will matter. People don't really want to live forever. Living forever would be like reading a good book, or watching a good movie, that never ended.

People understand that the story of their lives has to have a beginning, a middle, and an end. But what they desperately want is to live long enough to get it right, to feel that they have done something worthwhile with their lives, however long.

The author Milan Kundera has written, "Everyone has trouble accepting the fact that he will disappear, unheard of and unnoticed in an indifferent universe." When Mark Twain has Tom Sawyer attend his own funeral and listen to the eulogies of people who think he has died, I think he is tapping into a universal fantasy that at our funerals we will hear people speak of how much they miss us and we will be comforted that our lives made a difference. Some people strive to do great things, or terrible things, to make sure that they are noticed in life and remembered after death. Others turn to religion for the reassurance that the universe is not indifferent.

Jacob lived out his last years in comfort, settling in Egypt, where his favorite son was an important government official, surrounded by children and grandchildren. Then, one day, as we read in chapter 48 of Genesis, he sends a message to Joseph, "Behold, your father is ill." A Jewish tradition fastens on the detail that Jacob is the first person in the Bible to be described as being ill. It imagines a world where people did not get sick or become feeble as they grew older. They lived and lived and lived until one day they sneezed, their souls flew out their noses, and they died (which is why, to this day, we say "Gesundheit" or "God bless you" when someone sneezes). Jacob prayed to God to give him advance warning of his impending death, so that he would have time to get his affairs in order and prepare his family for life without him.

Joseph comes to visit his father, and Jacob reminisces about his life. He has lived a long time. In an age when most people never traveled beyond the confines of their native village, he has lived in three countries. He has known wealth and poverty, triumph and loss. But as he looks back over his whole life, two memories stand out. He remembers the night when God appeared to him and assured him that, despite his faults and his failings, he would grow up to be a good person and make a difference to the world. And he remembers that once he knew what it felt like to truly love someone. That someone, his wife Rachel, Joseph's mother, had died many years earlier, but Jacob has learned that love and memory are stronger than death, and her memory has remained with him every day since then.

It seems to me that Jacob got it right. Goodness and love are two of the experiences that assure us that our lives have mattered to the world, that we have not lived in vain. Jacob could contemplate with profound satisfaction how he overcame early mistakes and moral compromises to become a good man, and how his being a good man made a difference. He could not have foreseen that his descendants would give the world the Bible, the Ten Commandments, the prophets, and the Psalms. But he had every reason to believe that each person who chooses to be generous rather than selfish, to be truthful rather than deceptive, represents a vote for a world of generosity and truth rather than selfishness and deception. If enough people vote that way, we will end up with a more generous, more truthful community, and we will all benefit.

The young Jacob believed that, in order to make his mark on the world, he had to take advantage of people—his blind father, his hungry and unsophisticated brother. He thought that if he could find the other person's weakness and exploit it he would win and his rival would lose. But when Laban recognized Jacob's weakness, his love for Rachel, and used that weakness to cheat and exploit him, everything changed for Jacob. He looked at Laban and felt as if he were looking at himself in a mirror, and he didn't like what he saw. Jacob is, at his core, a decent person who does not to want people to think ill of him as he has come to think ill of Laban, as a man who will do anything to get the better of another, even his own nephew and son-in-law. And he does not want to live in the kind of world we would create if everyone behaved as Laban did.

There is an old folktale about the village that was planning a gala New Year's Eve celebration. Every inhabitant of the village was asked to contribute a bottle of wine, pouring it into a giant vat in the town square. On New Year's Eve, the vat would be available to everyone, to drink and usher in the new year. At midnight, the town fathers opened the spigots and invited the people to share the wine, but when they raised their glasses, they found them filled with water. Everyone in town had had the same idea: If all my neighbors bring wine, nobody will notice if I bring a bottle of water instead. In a town full of Labans, everyone cheats, and as a result, everyone is cheated. Just as liars are believed only because most people tell the truth, connivers count on the honesty and decency of their neighbors for their schemes to succeed. Good people hope that others will act as they do, whereas the Labans of the world hope that only they are clever enough and ruthless enough to get away with their schemes. If everyone acted as they did, everyone would end up as unhappy as everyone else. Good people may not generate headlines for their good behavior, but every vote for a decent society counts.

Jacob learned the lesson that others don't have to lose for you to win, and that you don't have to do great things, headline-grabbing deeds, to matter to the world. Everyone who puts in an honest day's work, everyone who goes out of his or her way to help a neighbor, everyone who makes a child laugh, changes the world for the better.

We have seen the slow but inexorable progression of human society from having one person, the king, determine the course of people's lives to having people vote to decide things for themselves. But we don't vote only in elections. The small choices and decisions we make a hundred times a day add up to determining the kind of world we live in.

I read the spy novels of John le Carré for their fiendishly clever plots and for their insights into the morally ambiguous world of international espionage. Whereas most spy novels pit virtuous good guys against unspeakably evil villains, le Carré's heroes are flawed, fallible human beings whose goodness is shown in their lack of certainty about a world where right and wrong are not always clear. I admire le Carré's writing and character development, and I appreciate why his endings are often morally ambiguous. But only once have I been emotionally moved by a le Carré novel. *Smiley's People* pits le Carré's British protagonist, George Smiley, against his Russian nemesis, a man named Karla. Karla has always gotten the better of Smiley, has always been a step ahead, always a little bit more clever. But Smiley learns that Karla has a mentally ill daughter and has diverted some of his espionage budget to get her into a sanitorium in Switzerland, in violation of Soviet law. Smiley gets a message to Karla: If he will defect to the British, they will see to it that his daughter continues to receive first-rate care. If he does not, Smiley will arrange for the Soviet government to find out what Karla has been doing behind their backs. The novel ends with Karla crossing over to the British side.

Did the good guys win? Smiley has based his life on the premise that the world will be better off if Great Britain outdoes Soviet Russia in intelligence gathering, and I and most of his readers would agree with that. But in order to make that happen, in the messy and morally ambiguous world of international intrigue, he has won by taking advantage of his opponent's love for his child. Le Carré teases us with the question: Who is the good person here and who is the villain? In the novel's last lines, Smiley is congratulated by a colleague: "George, you won." And he answers, "Did I? Yes, well, I suppose I did." But he is clearly uneasy. Would the world be a better place with more Smileys, acting cruelly on behalf of democracy, or with more Karlas, loving a vulnerable child more than they love winning?

This brings us to Jacob's second enduring memory: His life has not been a failure, his life has not been meaningless, because at least once in that life he knew what it felt like to love someone.

Years ago, when I was struggling with the question of why bad things happen to good people, I read Thornton Wilder's 1927 novel *The Bridge of San Luis Rey*. Wilder was also deeply concerned with the issue of good people suffering. His book tells of a rope bridge over a deep gorge in a small Peruvian village that suddenly collapses, sending five people to their deaths. A young Catholic priest, Brother Juniper, witnesses the tragedy and becomes obsessed with the question of why God would let it happen. He researches the lives of the five unrelated, seemingly random victims and learns that each of them had recently resolved a relationship issue in his or her life, and each of them had learned what it means to love someone. Brother Juniper's conclusion: We are put here on earth to learn to love, and when we have done that, we have fulfilled our life's mission. The book concludes: "Soon we shall die and all memory of those five will have left the earth.

We ourselves shall be loved for a while and forgotten. But the love will have been enough. . . . There is a land of the living and a land of the dead, and the bridge is love, the only survival, the only meaning."

Jacob, coming to the end of his life, is saying, in effect: When I was young, I wanted to change the world. I wanted to be so important that everyone would know my name. I may not have done that, but along the way, I loved someone. I changed her life and she changed mine, and that meant everything. That made it all worthwhile.

If you have ever attended the funeral of a person who died young or died tragically, perhaps the victim of a crime, a drunk driver, an accident that didn't have to happen, you will recognize one phrase that is virtually always used in the eulogy: We have to do something so that this person we loved and lost will not have died in vain. Our souls rebel at the thought that a good person's life, because it was short, was meaningless, so we insist on giving it meaning. Whether it be a call for new laws or for more medical research, we need to reassure ourselves that we can make something good come out of the tragedy. We can just barely accept the fact that good people die too soon. It is too much for us to think that their lives may have been wasted.

I believe in turning tragedy into the foundation stone of something good and life-enhancing. I have worked hard to do that myself. But whether we succeed in that effort or not, whether or not new laws are passed and new research is funded, no life is ever wasted. If a person has known love, has felt and given love, that person's life has made a difference.

Alice McDermott's novel *Charming Billy* describes an Irish-American family mourning the death of their lovable, hardworking, hard-drinking brother, husband, and friend. At one point, the widow says to a priest who has come to comfort them, "It's a terrible thing, Father, to come this far in life only to find that nothing you've felt has made any difference." The priest answers, "Of course it mattered. Everything you felt, everything you did for Billy mattered, regardless of how it turned out."

When we have loved someone and that person dies, what happens to all the love we invested in that person? The Israeli poet Yehuda Amichai offers a bold and arresting image to answer that question. He suggests that a person's body absorbs and stores all the love it receives in the course of a lifetime, from parents, from lovers, from husbands or wives, from children and friends. Then, when the body dies, it pours out all that love "like a broken slot machine disgorging the coins of all the generations," and all the people nearby, and all the world, are warmed by the love that has been returned to them. People die, but love does not die. It is recycled from one heart, from one life, to another. Jacob, decades after he met Rachel and fell in love with her, decades after her tragic death, is still warmed by the memory of that love, the love he gave and the love he received.

There is one more way in which Jacob reassures himself

that his life has mattered, that the world is a better place for his having lived. He doesn't list it among his memories, because it is not a memory. It comes not out of his past but out of his hopes for the future. Near the end of the book of Genesis, after Jacob has reminisced about his life, he gathers his children and grandchildren to his bedside and blesses them. He praises each of them for their good qualities and chastises them for their moral failings. But throughout his last speech to them, he makes it clear that what he is expressing is a combination of concern for their happiness and well-being and concern for his vicarious immortality. What he has learned, what he has come to stand for, will not die with him but will live on in the children he raised and the values he imparted to them. "May the Lord who has led me all my life long to this day bless these children, and in them may my name be perpetuated." (Genesis 48:15–16.) It was for this moment that he prayed to God to give him advance warning that his time was coming to an end, that he might share these last thoughts with those who would carry his name, his memory, and his values into the next generation.

We began this book by noting the conflict between conscience and success, between the wish to be a good person and the thirst to have an impact on the world. We discovered that there need not be a conflict. By being good people, by bringing good people together to form moral communities, we have an impact on the world.

We began by wondering how much of a difference one

person can make in a world whose population numbers in the billions. We saw that love and goodness matter more than we might have imagined. The dream of the ladder gave Jacob the gift of hope, the promise that he could climb higher than where he was at the moment, that he would not always be the ethically compromised, morally conflicted person he was then. The struggle with the angel gave him the blessing of integrity, bringing peace to his divided soul by making God's values his values. And marriage and parenthood offered him the promise of immortality, the vision that the things he had learned and come to stand for would live on beyond his life.

May I end this book on a personal note? I am at a point in my life where the years behind me far outnumber the years ahead. Like Jacob, I can look back with satisfaction at the path along which God has led me. Like Jacob, I have wrestled with the better angels of my nature, tried to resist them, and ultimately learned the wisdom and the blessing of letting the angel win. Like Jacob, I have known success and I have known disappointment, with the good years far outnumbering the bad ones. I have prayed, in the words of the psalmist, "Teach me to feel joy as deeply as I feel sorrow" (Psalm 90:15), and my prayer was answered. Like Jacob, I have known the experience of losing someone whom I loved more desperately than life itself, and remembering that person and that love every day of my life afterward. Like Jacob, I discovered in myself a strength I did not know I had until the day I needed it, a strength built upon the rock of the memory of that love. And, like Jacob, I find myself today surrounded by family (I am more fortunate than Jacob in that I have my wife with me) to love me and be loved by me.

When all of us come face to face with our mortality, either because of the accumulation of years or because we have seen names and numbers in the obituary pages that strike uncomfortably close to home, people like me who write books have an advantage over other people. For at least a while after my time is over, my books will still have a place on library shelves and in people's homes. More than that, the survival of my ideas and my values (much more the real me than my physical body) will rest with the people who write me letters and come up to me after my lectures to tell me what my books have meant to them.

But in the final analysis, the key to my immortality, the reassurance that my life has mattered and was not lived in vain, is not that different from the key to yours or anyone else's. I find it in the work I have done, the acts of kindness I have performed, the love I have given and the love I have received, the people who will smile when they remember me, and the children and grandchildren through whom my name and memory will be perpetuated. I have cherished, and I would commend to you, the words of Ralph Waldo Emerson: "To leave the world a bit better, whether by a healthy child, a garden patch, or a redeemed social condition; to know that even one life has breathed easier because you lived—that is to have succeeded."

The Talmud records this exchange between two of the sages:

"Our ancestor Jacob never died."

"How can you say that? The Bible describes him as dying in Egypt and being buried in Hebron."

"A good person, even in death, is still alive."

AFTERWORD

This book was first published in hardcover on September 4, 2001. One week later, our world changed as terrorists commandeered four airplanes and crashed them into the two buildings of the World Trade Center in New York, the Pentagon in Washington, and a field in Pennsylvania, causing the deaths of thousands of innocent people who just happened to be working in the wrong place or flying to the wrong destination at the wrong time. For those generations for which Pearl Harbor has been a page in a history book, life would never be the same. Americans would now have to live with that same sense of vulnerability that people in Israel, Colombia, Northern Ireland, and too many places on earth have had to live with.

What have we learned about ourselves and our world in the aftermath of the events of September 11th, and what light can the ideas set forth in this book shed on those events?

Among the most poignant stories to come out of the tragedy were the accounts of what people did when they realized that they might have only minutes to live. Nobody called his office. Nobody called his broker. Everyone without exception called his or her family. Almost universally, their last words were "If I don't make it out of here alive, I just want you to know I love you and I love the kids." The victims of September 11th, in the air and on the ground, included high-level business executives and minimum-wage kitchen workers, but in the searing crucible of impending death, they all realized what they might not have understood as clearly before: nothing matters more to us than our families and the people we love. Not our jobs, not our investments, not our plans for the future.

The primary focus of this book is the human need for significance, the assurance that we matter to the world. And its conclusion is that the most reliable way to matter to the world is to love the people closest to us, our mates, our children, our families, our closest friends. Our love changes them even as the ability to love changes us, even as our inviting and accepting their love changes them and changes us as well.

If there is any good to be derived from the terrible events of September 2001, it may be the rediscovery of the power and importance of love. So many people think that the secret of making one's mark on the world lies in outdoing our competitors, finding their weakness and exploiting it. Perhaps we will learn from these tragedies that we leave our mark on the world not by defeating others but by reaching out to them. As we learned more about the people who died in the plane crashes and the collapsed buildings, I was struck by the fact that virtually no one spoke of their business achievements. No one spoke of how much money they had made in their lives. One after another, people spoke of what loving husbands and fathers they had been, what special mothers and wives, what good friends. They spoke of what the victims had done for their communities, what they had given rather than what they had taken. If we would be remembered as affectionately and with as much admiration as they were, let that be the focus of our lives as well. The Jackson Browne song has it right: "Nothing survives / But the way we live our lives."

I don't like feeling vulnerable to terrorist threats. I liked it much better when I could take refuge in the notion of American exceptionalism. It felt good to believe that geography—being surrounded by oceans east and west and friendly neighbors north and south—and morality—we are a good, generous people—would keep us safe from the dangers that afflicted so many other countries. But that faith is gone now.

Is there anything good to say about this feeling of vulnerability? Perhaps there is. Let me suggest that *faith in God begins where human self-sufficiency ends*. When we realize that we can do many marvelous things but we can't do everything, and especially that we can't control the most important things, then we recognize our need to turn to God. In the Bible, idolatry is not a matter of praying to stones and statues. Idolatry is worshipping the work of our own hands, treating the human being and the human mind as the highest source of value in the world. Only when we confront things that we cannot control—issues of war and peace, health and illness, habits too strong for our willpower to change—do we find ourselves turning to God.

America at the dawn of the twenty-first century verged on being an idolatrous country. We claimed to believe in God, but too often we tended to *use* God rather than to *serve* God. We assumed that, if we knew the right words and performed the right deeds, we could control God for our purposes much as we had learned to control fire, electricity, nuclear energy, and other awesomely powerful forces. One wishes that the lesson might have been learned less expensively, but it seems that on September 11th, we were reminded that the most important things in our lives, peace and love and life itself, are beyond our power to guarantee.

Among the thousands who died as a result of the crimes of September 11th, several hundred were in a different category than the rest. The airplane passengers, the office workers had no choice; they were caught up in events beyond their control. But the hundreds of New York City police and firefighters who died, and the hundreds more who survived, chose to put their lives at risk to try to save other lives. In doing so, they gave us the answer to what otherwise might have been an embarrassing question: our enemies believed strongly enough in their cause to die for it. Do we believe equally strongly in ours?

Six weeks after the tragedy, the first game of the World Series was played in Phoenix. Ray Charles was invited to sing the national anthem. He chose to pass over the "Star-Spangled Banner" and sang "America the Beautiful" instead, offering the seldom-heard third verse:

"O beautiful for heroes proved in liberating strife
    Who more than self the country loved,
    and mercy more than life."

As I heard those words, I could not stop the tears from flowing as I thought of the heroes of September 11th who "loved . . . mercy more than life" and reminded us of the capacity for altruism and sacrifice, the unselfish love for strangers in need, of which human beings at their best are capable.

The worlds of commerce, air travel, warfare, and international relations have been changed irreparably by the events of September 11th. Because religion is such a basic ingredient of the way we view our world, religion will inevitably have been affected as well. The early responses were troubling.

There was much scapegoating of Islam as a whole rather than Islamic fanatics. In addition to isolated acts of violence against Muslims, a prominent Christian clergyman called Islam "an evil religion." I was on a television panel with a Protestant cleric who insisted that, of the thousands who died in the attack, only those who believed in Jesus would end up in Heaven. But as the shock and anger of those first days faded, cooler heads prevailed and more and more, we came to realize that the villain was not Islam but fanaticism, and that all religions are vulnerable to that sin. We came to understand that the only kind of religion that deserves to flourish in the twenty-first century is not the one that says "my way is God's way" but the one that reaches out a hand of fellowship and says "despite our theological differences, we are all in this quest together." But it has been a long, slow climb for religion to outgrow its contentious path and reach that point.

Why, for some people, does religious faith metastasize into religious fanaticism? Perhaps because there are some people who cling so desperately to their faith that they cannot accept the possibility that they are wrong and someone else may be right. They have invested too much of themselves emotionally in what they believe.

Remember that Islam is less than 1,400 years old. When Judaism was 1,200 years old, it was converting the inhabitants of captured territories by force. When Christianity was 1,200 to 1,400 years old, it was graduating from the bloodshed of the Crusades to the tortures of the Inquisition. It may be that a world religion has to go through an "adolescent" phase of believing that it has the total truth (plausibly, as in so many adolescents, a cover for insecurity; why else would a worldwide religious organization be so panicked at the thought of a roomful of heretics somewhere in its domain?) before it matures.

Truth be told, it is only in the last fifty years or so that Christians and Jews have learned to speak to each other, seeking to learn from one another rather than disprove one another's theologies. When I was growing up in Brooklyn in the 1940s and 50s, my rabbi was a national leader of the American Jewish community. I suspect he did not know a single Christian clergyman on a first-name basis. Back then, Catholic priests claimed that "error has no rights" and forbade their parishioners to attend non-Catholic services. Back then, rabbis and ministers were more likely to speak to those of their own faith about how everyone else was wrong than to actually meet those "everyone else" in the fullness of their faith. In the ensuing decades, we have come to understand that God's heart is big enough to embrace all of God's children, and there is every reason to believe that Islam will become part of that process in the future as well.

One question remains to be confronted as we ponder the impact of September 11th on people's faith: Where was God? How could God let so many innocent people die so horribly? I was frequently asked that question in the wake of the attacks, and my answer was and is that God's promise was never that life would be fair. The suffering and death of innocent people has shadowed our world long before September 11th. God's promise was that when we have to confront the pain and unfairness of the world, we would not have to do it alone for He would be with us.

Do we yearn to matter to the world? We matter, not because of our achievements but because we are loved by God and loved by the people around us. That love may not shield us from pain, death, and loss, but it will make them more bearable, and that will be enough.